Scroll No More: Breaking Free from Phone Addiction

A Practical Guide to Overcoming Smartphone Addiction

L.Harris Spike

L.Harris Spike

Table of Contents

Dedication

To everyone who feels trapped in the glow of their screen,

May this book guide you toward freedom, presence, and a life that's truly your

own. This is for the moments you've been missing and the connections that

matter most.

*"The chains of habit are too weak to be felt until they are
too strong to be broken."*

- Samuel Johnson

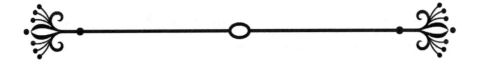

Introduction

◆ <u>Why We Need a Breakup</u>

Let's face it: our phones have become more than just tools. They're our constant companions, our go-to for entertainment, and our escape from boredom. But somewhere along the way, this relationship turned toxic. We've become so attached to our devices that we've lost sight of what really matters—our mental health, our relationships, and our ability to live in the moment. It's time to take a step back and ask ourselves: *Is this really how we want to live?*

The numbers don't lie. According to a 2023 report by DataReportal, the average person spends **7 hours a day** on their phone. That's almost half of our waking hours! And it's not just adults—teens are spending even more time glued to their screens, with some studies showing up to **9 hours a day**. When you add it all up, that's over **2,500 hours a year** spent scrolling, swiping, and tapping. Imagine what we could do with that time if we weren't so tied to our devices.

But it's not just about the time we lose. Phone addiction has real consequences for our mental health. A study published in the *Journal of Social and Clinical Psychology* found that people who spent more time on social media reported higher levels of anxiety, depression, and loneliness. Why? Because constantly comparing ourselves to others online can make us feel inadequate. We see curated versions of people's lives—perfect vacations, flawless selfies, and endless achievements—and we start to wonder why our own lives don't measure up. This cycle of comparison can lead to feelings of worthlessness and even contribute to mental health issues.

And let's not forget the impact on our relationships. Have you ever been out to dinner with friends or family, only to realize everyone is staring at their phones instead of talking to each other? You're not alone. A survey by the Pew Research Center found that **89% of people** admitted to using their phones during their last social gathering. This constant distraction makes it harder to connect with the people right in front of us. Over time, it can even damage our closest relationships. Think about it: how many meaningful conversations have been cut short because someone got a notification?

Then there's the toll on our productivity. Our phones are designed to distract us, and they're really good at it. Every time we get a notification, our focus is pulled away from what we're doing. Research from the University of California, Irvine, found that it takes an average of **23 minutes** to get back on track after a distraction. That means every time you check your phone, you're losing almost half an hour of productive time. Over the course of a day, those interruptions add up, leaving us feeling overwhelmed and unaccomplished.

But perhaps the most heartbreaking cost of phone addiction is the moments we miss. When we're constantly glued to our screens, we're not fully present in our own lives. We miss the little things— the sound of birds chirping, the smile on a loved one's face, or the feeling of the sun on our skin. These moments may seem small, but they're the ones that make life meaningful. And once they're gone, we can't get them back.

So, why do we need a breakup with our phones? Because they're taking more from us than they're giving. They're stealing our time, our mental health, our relationships, and our ability to be present. But here's the good news: it doesn't have to be this way. We can take control of our relationship with technology and create a healthier balance. It won't be easy—breaking up never is—but it's worth it. Because on the other side of this breakup is a life that's more focused, more connected, and more fulfilling.

Let's take a look at some key stats to drive the point home:

Statistic	Details
Average daily phone usage	7 hours (DataReportal, 2023)

Teens' daily screen time	Up to 9 hours (Common Sense Media, 2022)
Time lost to distractions	23 minutes to refocus after a distraction (University of California, 2018)
People using phones during social time	89% (Pew Research Center, 2021)
Mental health impact	Higher anxiety, depression, and loneliness (Journal of Social Psychology)

These numbers paint a clear picture: our phones are controlling us more than we realize. But it's not too late to change. By recognizing the problem and taking steps to reduce our dependency, we can reclaim our time, our focus, and our lives. The first step is admitting that we need a breakup. The next step is making it happen.

♦ The Hidden Costs of Phone Addiction

When we think about phone addiction, the first thing that comes to mind is wasted time. We know we spend hours scrolling through social media, watching videos, or checking emails. But the truth is, the cost of phone addiction goes much deeper than just lost time. There are hidden costs—emotional, mental, and even physical—that we often don't see until it's too late. These costs are quietly chipping away at our well-being, relationships, and even our ability to think clearly. Let's take a closer look at what we're really losing.

1. Mental Health: The Silent Toll

One of the biggest hidden costs of phone addiction is its impact on our mental health. Studies show that excessive phone use, especially on social media, is linked to higher levels of anxiety, depression, and loneliness. For example, a 2022 study by the *American Psychological Association* found that people who spent more than **2 hours a day** on social media were **three times more likely** to feel depressed than those who spent less time online. Why? Because social media often makes us feel like we're not good enough. We compare our lives to the highlight reels of others, and it leaves us feeling empty.

But it's not just social media. Even the constant notifications from our phones can keep our brains in a state of stress. Every buzz, beep, or ping triggers a small release of cortisol, the stress hormone. Over time, this constant state of alertness can lead to chronic stress, which has been linked to a host of health problems, including heart disease and weakened immune systems.

2. Relationships: The Distance Between Us

Our phones are supposed to connect us, but ironically, they often drive us apart. Think about the last time you were with friends or family. Were you fully present, or were you half-listening while scrolling through your phone? A survey by *Pew Research Center* found that **51% of people** say their partner is distracted by their phone during conversations. This "phubbing" (phone snubbing) can lead to feelings of neglect and resentment, damaging even the strongest relationships.

And it's not just romantic relationships that suffer. Parents who are glued to their phones may miss out on meaningful moments with their children. A study published in *Child Development* found that children whose parents were frequently on their phones felt less important and more disconnected. These small moments of distraction add up, creating a gap between us and the people we care about most.

3. Productivity: The Myth of Multitasking

We like to think we're good at multitasking, but the truth is, our brains aren't built for it. Every time we switch between tasks—like answering a text while working—we lose focus. Research from the *University of London* found that multitasking with our phones can lower our IQ by up to **15 points**, similar to the effect of losing a night's sleep. Over time, this constant switching makes it harder to concentrate, leading to lower productivity and more mistakes.

And it's not just work that suffers. Even our hobbies and creative pursuits take a hit. When we're constantly interrupted by our phones, we lose the ability to dive deep into activities that require focus, like reading, painting, or playing music. This not only robs us of joy but also stifles our creativity.

4. Physical Health: The Body Pays the Price

Phone addiction doesn't just affect our minds—it takes a toll on our bodies too. Spending hours hunched over our screens can lead to "tech neck," a condition caused by poor posture that results in neck and back pain. According to a study by *Harvard Medical School,* **58% of smartphone users** report experiencing neck or shoulder pain due to prolonged phone use.

Then there's the impact on our sleep. The blue light emitted by our phones interferes with the production of melatonin, the hormone that helps us sleep. A study by the *National Sleep Foundation* found that **90% of people** use their phones within an hour of bedtime, and **60%** say it affects their sleep quality. Poor sleep, in turn, affects everything from our mood to our immune system.

5. Missed Moments: The Cost of Being Disconnected

Perhaps the most heartbreaking cost of phone addiction is the moments we miss. When we're glued to our screens, we're not fully present in our own lives. We miss the little things—the sound of laughter, the beauty of a sunset, or the joy of a spontaneous conversation. These moments may seem small, but they're the ones that make life meaningful. And once they're gone, we can't get them back.

Key Stats at a Glance

Hidden Cost	Details
Mental Health Impact	3x higher risk of depression with >2 hours of social media use (APA, 2022)
Relationship Strain	51% of people feel their partner is distracted by their phone (Pew, 2021)
Productivity Loss	Multitasking lowers IQ by 15 points (University of London, 2015)
Physical Health Issues	58% of users experience neck/shoulder pain (Harvard Medical School, 2020)
Sleep Disruption	90% use phones before bed; 60% report poor sleep (National Sleep Foundation)

The hidden costs of phone addiction are real, and they're affecting every part of our lives. But the good news is, we don't have to accept this as our reality.

◆ <u>What "Phone Canceling" Really Means</u>

Let's get one thing straight: "phone canceling" doesn't mean throwing your phone in the trash and never looking back. That's not realistic, and it's not the point. What it *does* mean is taking back control. It's about breaking free from the hold your phone has on your life and creating a healthier, more intentional relationship with technology. Think of it like this: your phone should work for *you*, not the other way around.

So, what does "phone canceling" look like in real life? It's about setting boundaries. It's about deciding when, where, and how you use your phone—and sticking to those decisions. It's about recognizing that your time, attention, and mental health are more valuable than any notification or social media post.

1. It's Not About Quitting Cold Turkey

Let's be honest: most of us can't just quit our phones completely. We need them for work, staying in touch with loved ones, and even navigating the world. "Phone canceling" isn't about giving up your phone entirely; it's about using it more mindfully. For example, instead of mindlessly scrolling through Instagram for an hour, you might set a timer for 10 minutes and then put your phone down. Small changes like this can make a big difference over time.

2. It's About Taking Back Your Time

Did you know that the average person checks their phone **58 times a day**? That's according to a 2023 study by Asurion. And each time you pick up your phone, you're losing focus and wasting precious time. "Phone canceling" means being intentional about how you spend your time. It's about asking yourself: *Is this really how I want to spend my day?* If the answer is no, it's time to make a change.

One way to do this is by setting specific times for checking your phone. For example, you might decide to check your email and social media only three times a day—morning, afternoon, and evening. The rest of the time, your phone stays out of sight. This simple habit can help you reclaim hours of your day and reduce the constant distraction.

3. It's About Protecting Your Mental Health

Your phone can be a source of stress, anxiety, and even depression. The constant notifications, the pressure to respond immediately, and the endless comparison on social media can take a toll on your mental health. "Phone canceling" means creating a space where you can breathe and focus on what really matters.

For example, you might turn off non-essential notifications or use "Do Not Disturb" mode during certain times of the day. A 2021 study by the *University of British Columbia* found that people who limited their social media use to **30 minutes a**

day reported significant improvements in their mood and overall well-being. That's the power of setting boundaries.

4. It's About Being Present

How many times have you been in a conversation with someone, only to realize you've been half-listening because you're distracted by your phone? "Phone canceling" means being fully present in the moment. It's about putting your phone away during meals, when you're spending time with loved ones, or when you're doing something you enjoy.

A survey by *BankMyCell* found that **71% of people** feel that their phone distracts them from being present in their daily lives. By setting boundaries with your phone, you can reclaim those moments and truly connect with the people and experiences around you.

5. It's About Rediscovering What Matters

At its core, "phone canceling" is about prioritizing what really matters in your life. It's about making space for the things that bring you joy—whether that's spending time with family, pursuing a hobby, or simply enjoying a quiet moment alone. When you reduce the noise and distraction of your phone, you create room for the things that truly matter.

Key Stats at a Glance

What "Phone Canceling" Means	Details
Average daily phone checks	58 times (Asurion, 2023)
Social media use and mental health	30 minutes/day improves mood (University of British Columbia, 2021)
Phone distractions	71% feel phones distract them from being present (BankMyCell, 2020)
Time saved by setting boundaries	Reclaim hours/day by limiting phone use

How to Start "Phone Canceling" Today

1. **Set Boundaries**: Decide when and where you'll use your phone. For example, no phones during meals or after 8 p.m.

2. **Turn Off Notifications**: Only allow essential notifications (like calls and texts) to come through.

3. **Create Phone-Free Zones**: Designate certain areas, like your bedroom or dining room, as phone-free zones.

4. **Use Tools to Help You**: Apps like Freedom or Forest can help you stay focused by blocking distracting apps.

5. **Be Kind to Yourself**: If you slip up, don't beat yourself up. Just refocus and try again.

"Phone canceling" isn't about perfection. It's about progress. It's about taking small steps to create a healthier relationship with your phone and, in turn, a more fulfilling life.

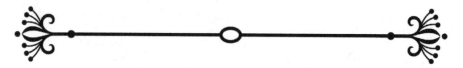

Chapter 1: The Problem

1.1 How We Got Hooked

◆ The Evolution of the Smartphone

Let's take a trip down memory lane. Remember when phones were just... phones? They fit in your pocket, had physical buttons, and their sole purpose was to make calls and send texts. Fast forward to today, and smartphones are more like mini-computers. They're our cameras, our maps, our entertainment systems, and even our personal assistants. But how did we get here? And more importantly, how did these devices go from being simple tools to something we can't seem to live without? Let's break it down.

The Early Days: From Brick Phones to Flip Phones

The first mobile phones were far from smart. In the 1980s, they were big, bulky, and expensive. The Motorola DynaTAC 8000X, one of the first mobile phones, weighed **2.2 pounds** and cost **3,995**∗∗(that's over∗∗**3,995**∗∗(*that's over*∗∗**10,000** in today's money!). It could only make calls, and the battery lasted about 30 minutes. But despite their limitations, these "brick phones" were a game-changer. For the first time, people could make calls from anywhere.

By the 1990s, phones got smaller and more affordable. Flip phones like the Motorola Razr became popular. They were sleek, stylish, and still pretty basic. You could make calls, send texts, and maybe play a simple game like Snake. But that was about it. Phones were still just tools, not the center of our lives.

The Smartphone Revolution

Everything changed in 2007 when Apple introduced the iPhone. This wasn't just a phone—it was a mini-computer with a touchscreen, internet access, and apps. Suddenly, you could check your email, browse the web, and even watch videos on your phone. Other companies quickly followed suit, and smartphones became the new norm.

But here's the thing: smartphones weren't just designed to make our lives easier. They were designed to keep us hooked. Features like push notifications, endless scrolling, and app updates were created to grab and hold our attention. And it worked. By 2010, the average person was spending **2.7 hours a day** on their phone. Today, that number has more than doubled to **7 hours a day**, according to a 2023 report by DataReportal.

The Rise of the Attention Economy

As smartphones became more advanced, companies realized they could make money by keeping us glued to our screens. This is what's known as the "attention economy." Apps like Facebook, Instagram, and TikTok are designed to keep you scrolling for as long as possible. The more time you spend on their platforms, the more ads you see, and the more money they make.

But the cost of this attention economy is high. A 2022 study by the *Journal of Social and Clinical Psychology* found that people who spent more than **2 hours a day** on social media were **three times more likely** to feel depressed or anxious. The constant stream of information, notifications, and updates can overwhelm our brains and leave us feeling drained.

The Smartphone Today: A Double-Edged Sword

Today's smartphones are more powerful than ever. They can do almost anything—navigate us to a new city, track our fitness, and even pay for our groceries. But with all this power comes a price. Our phones have become so addictive that many of us feel like we can't live without them. A 2021 survey by *BankMyCell* found that **71% of people** feel anxious when they're separated from their phones. That's not healthy.

Key Stats at a Glance

Era	Key Milestones
1980s	First mobile phones (e.g., Motorola DynaTAC 8000X) – heavy, expensive, basic
1990s	Flip phones (e.g., Motorola Razr) – sleek, affordable, still basic

2007	iPhone introduced – touchscreen, apps, internet access
2010	Average phone use: 2.7 hours/day
2023	Average phone use: 7 hours/day (DataReportal)
Social Media Impact	>2 hours/day on social media = 3x higher risk of depression (Journal of Psychology)
Phone Separation Anxiety	71% feel anxious without their phone (BankMyCell, 2021)

Where Do We Go From Here?

The evolution of the smartphone has brought us incredible convenience, but it's also created new challenges. Our phones are no longer just tools—they're constant companions that demand our attention. But here's the good news: we don't have to let them control us. By understanding how smartphones evolved and why they're designed to be addictive, we can start to take back control.

It's time to rethink our relationship with these devices. Instead of letting them dictate our lives, we can use them intentionally and mindfully. That might mean setting boundaries, turning off notifications, or even taking regular breaks from our screens. The choice is ours.

So, the next time you pick up your phone, ask yourself: *Is this serving me, or am I serving it?* The answer might surprise you.

◆ The Psychology of Addiction: Why We Can't Put It Down

Have you ever told yourself, "I'll just check my phone for a minute," only to look up an hour later, wondering where the time went? You're not alone. Many of us struggle to put our phones down, even when we know we should. But why is it so hard? The answer lies in the psychology of addiction. Our phones—and the apps on them—are designed to keep us hooked. Let's break it down so you can understand what's really going on.

1. The Dopamine Effect

At the heart of phone addiction is a chemical in your brain called **dopamine**. Dopamine is often called the "feel-good" chemical because it's released when we experience something pleasurable, like eating our favorite food or receiving a compliment. But here's the catch: dopamine isn't just about pleasure—it's about anticipation. It's what keeps us coming back for more.

Every time you get a notification, a like, or a new message, your brain gets a little hit of dopamine. It's like a mini-reward that makes you feel good, even if just for a moment. Over time, your brain starts to crave these hits, and you find yourself checking your phone more and more often. A 2020 study by *Harvard University* found that **80% of people** check their phones within **15 minutes** of waking up. That's how powerful this dopamine effect can be.

2. Variable Rewards: The Slot Machine Effect

Have you ever noticed how social media feeds are unpredictable? Sometimes you scroll for minutes without seeing anything interesting, and other times you stumble upon a funny meme or an exciting update. This unpredictability is by design. It's called **variable rewards**, and it's the same psychological trick used in slot machines.

When you don't know what you're going to get, your brain stays engaged, hoping for that next big reward. This keeps you scrolling, even when you know you should stop. A 2021 study by *Stanford University* found that people spend **2.5 times longer** on apps that use variable rewards compared to those that don't. That's why apps like Instagram, TikTok, and YouTube are so addictive—they're designed to keep you hooked.

3. Fear of Missing Out (FOMO)

Another reason we can't put our phones down is **FOMO**, or the fear of missing out. Social media makes it easy to see what everyone else is doing, and it's hard not to feel like you're missing something important. Whether it's a party you weren't invited to or a news story everyone's talking about, FOMO keeps us glued to our screens.

A 2022 survey by *BankMyCell* found that **69% of people** experience FOMO because of social media. This fear drives us to check our phones constantly, even when there's no real reason to. The problem is, the more we check, the more we feel like we're missing out, creating a vicious cycle.

4. The Infinite Scroll: No End in Sight

Ever notice how there's no "end" to your social media feed? That's not an accident. Apps like Facebook, Instagram, and Twitter use something called **infinite scroll**, which means there's always more content to see. There's no natural stopping point, so you just keep scrolling and scrolling.

This design feature taps into our brain's desire for completion. We want to see everything, but since there's no end, we never feel satisfied. A 2020 study by *Nielsen Norman Group* found that infinite scroll increases the time people spend on a site by **50%**. That's a lot of extra screen time.

5. Social Validation: The Like Button Trap

Finally, there's the issue of **social validation**. Every time someone likes your post or leaves a comment, it feels good. It's a sign that you're being seen and appreciated. But this need for validation can become addictive. A 2021 study by *UCLA* found that receiving likes on social media activates the same part of the brain as winning money or eating chocolate. That's why we keep posting and checking for reactions—it's like a little hit of happiness every time.

Key Stats at a Glance

Psychological Trick	Details
Dopamine Effect	80% check phones within 15 minutes of waking up (Harvard, 2020)
Variable Rewards	People spend 2.5x longer on apps with variable rewards (Stanford, 2021)
FOMO	69% experience FOMO due to social media (BankMyCell, 2022)
Infinite Scroll	Increases time spent on apps by 50% (Nielsen Norman Group, 2020)
Social Validation	Likes activate the brain's reward center (UCLA, 2021)

Breaking the Cycle

Now that you know why it's so hard to put your phone down, what can you do about it? Here are a few tips to help you break the cycle:

1. **Turn Off Notifications**: Reduce the dopamine hits by silencing non-essential alerts.

2. **Set Time Limits**: Use apps like Screen Time or Digital Wellbeing to limit your usage.

3. **Practice Mindfulness**: Be aware of when and why you're reaching for your phone.

4. **Create Phone-Free Zones**: Designate certain times or places where your phone isn't allowed.

5. **Focus on Real-Life Connections**: Spend more time with people in person, not just online.

◆ Big Tech and the Attention Economy

Let's talk about something that might make you a little uncomfortable: your phone isn't just a device—it's a product. And you're not just the user; you're also the product. Big Tech companies like Facebook, Google, and TikTok make billions of dollars by keeping you glued to your screen. How? By playing a game called the **attention economy**. In this game, your attention is the prize, and every app, notification, and algorithm is designed to win it. Let's break it down so you can see how it works—and how to take back control.

L.Harris Spike

What Is the Attention Economy?

The attention economy is simple: the more time you spend on an app or platform, the more money the company makes. How? Through ads. The longer you stay on Instagram, the more ads you see. The more videos you watch on YouTube, the more ads you're served. It's a business model built on keeping you engaged for as long as possible.

But here's the thing: your attention is limited. There are only so many hours in a day, and every company wants a piece of that time. That's why they use every trick in the book to keep you hooked. A 2023 report by *DataReportal* found that the average person spends **7 hours a day** on their phone. That's almost half of your waking hours! And Big Tech is cashing in. In 2022, Google and Facebook alone made over **$200 billion** from ads.

How Big Tech Keeps You Hooked

Big Tech companies use a mix of psychology, design, and technology to keep you coming back. Here are some of their most effective tricks:

1. **Push Notifications**: Every ping, buzz, or beep is designed to grab your attention. A 2021 study by *Dscout* found that the average person touches their phone **2,617 times a day**. That's not an accident—it's by design.

2. **Endless Scroll**: Apps like Instagram and TikTok use infinite scroll, meaning there's no natural stopping point. You just keep scrolling and scrolling, and before you know it, an hour has gone by. A 2020 study by *Nielsen Norman Group* found that infinite scroll increases time spent on apps by **50%**.

3. **Personalized Algorithms**: Ever notice how your social media feed seems to know exactly what you like? That's because algorithms track your every click, like, and scroll. They use this data to show you content that keeps you engaged. A 2022 study by *Stanford University* found that personalized algorithms can increase screen time by **30%**.

4. **Variable Rewards**: Apps are designed to give you unpredictable rewards—like a funny meme, a heartwarming story, or a viral video. This unpredictability keeps you coming back for more. A 2021 study by *Stanford University* found that people spend **2.5 times longer** on apps that use variable rewards.

The Cost of the Attention Economy

While Big Tech is raking in billions, the cost to us is high. The constant demand for our attention is taking a toll on our mental health, relationships, and productivity. A 2022 study by the *Journal of Social and Clinical Psychology* found that people who spend more than **2 hours a day** on social media are **three**

times more likely to feel depressed or anxious. And it's not just mental health—our relationships are suffering too. A survey by *BankMyCell* found that **71% of people** feel their phones distract them from being present in their daily lives.

Key Stats at a Glance

Big Tech's Tricks	Details
Average daily phone use	7 hours/day (DataReportal, 2023)
Google & Facebook ad revenue	$200 billion in 2022
Push notifications	Average person touches phone 2,617 times/day (Dscout, 2021)
Infinite scroll	Increases time spent on apps by 50% (Nielsen Norman Group, 2020)
Personalized algorithms	Increase screen time by 30% (Stanford, 2022)
Variable rewards	People spend 2.5x longer on apps with variable rewards (Stanford, 2021)

Mental health impact	>2 hours/day on social media = 3x higher risk of depression (Psychology)

How to Fight Back

Now that you know how the attention economy works, what can you do to protect your time and mental health? Here are a few tips:

1. **Turn Off Non-Essential Notifications**: Only allow alerts that are truly important, like calls or texts.

2. **Set Time Limits**: Use tools like Screen Time or Digital Wellbeing to limit how much time you spend on apps.

3. **Curate Your Feed**: Unfollow accounts that don't add value to your life, and mute or block content that stresses you out.

4. **Take Regular Breaks**: Schedule phone-free times during your day, like during meals or before bed.

5. **Be Mindful of Algorithms**: Remember, the content you see is designed to keep you hooked. Don't let it control you.

The attention economy is powerful, but it's not unbeatable. By understanding how Big Tech keeps you hooked, you can start to take back control of your time and attention. Remember, your attention is valuable—don't let anyone steal it without your permission.

1.2 Signs You're Addicted

♦ The Everyday Habits That Signal Dependence

Let's be honest: most of us don't realize how dependent we are on our phones until it's too late. We tell ourselves, "I'm just checking something real quick," or "I'll only scroll for a few minutes." But those quick checks and short scrolls add up, and before we know it, we're spending hours on our phones every day. The truth is, phone dependence doesn't happen overnight. It creeps up on us through small, everyday habits that we barely notice. But these habits are powerful, and they can take over our lives if we're not careful.

So, how do you know if you're dependent on your phone? Let's take a closer look at some of the most common habits that signal dependence. If you recognize yourself in any of these, don't worry—you're not alone, and there's always a way to break free.

1. Reaching for Your Phone First Thing in the Morning

Do you grab your phone as soon as you wake up, even before you get out of bed? If so, you're not alone. A 2023 survey by *Asurion* found that **80% of people** check their phones within **15 minutes** of waking up. For many of us, it's become a reflex—like brushing our teeth or making coffee.

But here's the problem: starting your day by scrolling through social media or checking emails can set a stressful tone for the rest of the day. Instead of easing into your morning, you're bombarded with notifications, news, and updates. This can leave you feeling overwhelmed before you've even had breakfast.

2. Checking Your Phone Constantly

Do you find yourself checking your phone every few minutes, even when you don't have a reason to? This is one of the most common signs of phone dependence. A 2021 study by *Dscout* found that the average person touches their phone **2,617 times a day**. That's a lot of unnecessary checking!

This habit is often driven by **FOMO** (fear of missing out). We're afraid that if we don't check our phones, we'll miss something important—a text from a friend, a work email, or a viral post. But the truth is, most of the time, there's nothing urgent waiting for us. We're just feeding our addiction.

3. Using Your Phone to Avoid Boredom

Do you pull out your phone every time you have a spare moment— waiting in line, sitting on the bus, or even during a commercial break? If so, you're using your phone as a way to avoid boredom. And while it might seem harmless, this habit can actually make it harder for your brain to relax and recharge.

A 2022 study by *The University of Virginia* found that people who couldn't sit alone with their thoughts for just **15 minutes** were more likely to feel anxious and stressed. Constantly filling every quiet moment with screen time prevents us from processing our thoughts and emotions, which can lead to mental health issues over time.

4. Feeling Anxious Without Your Phone

Do you feel uneasy or anxious when you don't have your phone with you? This is a classic sign of phone dependence. A 2021 survey by *BankMyCell* found that **71% of people** feel anxious when they're separated from their phones. Some people even experience physical symptoms, like a racing heart or sweaty palms.

This anxiety is often tied to the fear of missing out (FOMO). We worry that something important will happen while we're offline, and we'll be left out. But the truth is, most of the time, the world keeps turning just fine without us being constantly connected.

5. Using Your Phone During Social Interactions

Do you find yourself scrolling through your phone while you're with friends or family? This habit, known as **phubbing** (phone snubbing), is a major red flag for phone dependence. A 2021 survey by *Pew Research Center* found that **51% of people** say their partner is distracted by their phone during conversations.

Using your phone during social interactions sends a message that the person in front of you isn't as important as whatever's on your screen. Over time, this can damage relationships and make it harder to connect with others on a deeper level.

6. Losing Track of Time While Scrolling

Have you ever sat down to check your phone "for just a minute," only to look up and realize an hour has gone by? This is a common experience for many of us. A 2023 study by *DataReportal* found that the average person spends **7 hours a day** on their phone. That's almost half of your waking hours!

This habit is often fueled by **infinite scroll**, a design feature used by apps like Instagram and TikTok. There's no natural stopping point, so you just keep scrolling and scrolling, losing track of time in the process.

7. Using Your Phone to Escape Stress

Do you turn to your phone when you're feeling stressed or overwhelmed? Many of us use our phones as a way to escape negative emotions. Whether it's scrolling through social media, playing games, or watching videos, our phones provide a temporary distraction from our problems.

But here's the catch: while your phone might help you avoid stress in the short term, it often makes things worse in the long run. A 2022 study by the *Journal of Social and Clinical Psychology* found that people who used their phones to cope with stress were more likely to feel anxious and depressed over time.

8. Ignoring Real-Life Activities for Your Phone

Do you skip activities you used to enjoy—like reading, exercising, or spending time with loved ones—because you're too busy on your phone? This is a clear sign that your phone has taken over your life. A 2021 survey by *BankMyCell* found that **64% of people** said their phone use interfered with their hobbies and interests.

When we prioritize our phones over real-life activities, we miss out on the things that truly bring us joy and fulfillment. Over time, this can lead to feelings of emptiness and dissatisfaction.

Key Stats at a Glance

Habit	Details
Checking phone in the morning	80% check within 15 minutes of waking up (Asurion, 2023)
Constant phone checking	Average person touches phone 2,617 times/day (Dscout, 2021)
Avoiding boredom	People struggle to sit alone for 15 minutes (University of Virginia, 2022)
Anxiety without phone	71% feel anxious when separated from their phone (BankMyCell, 2021)

Phubbing	51% say their partner is distracted by their phone (Pew Research, 2021)
Losing track of time	Average person spends 7 hours/day on their phone (DataReportal, 2023)
Using phone to escape stress	Linked to higher anxiety and depression (Journal of Psychology, 2022)
Ignoring real-life activities	64% say phone use interferes with hobbies (BankMyCell, 2021)

Breaking the Cycle

If you recognize yourself in any of these habits, don't panic. The first step to breaking free from phone dependence is awareness. Once you know what's driving your behavior, you can start to make changes. Here are a few tips to help you get started:

1. **Set Boundaries**: Decide when and where you'll use your phone. For example, no phones during meals or after 8 p.m.

2. **Turn Off Notifications**: Only allow essential notifications (like calls and texts) to come through.

3. **Create Phone-Free Zones**: Designate certain areas, like your bedroom or dining room, as phone-free zones.

4. **Find Alternatives**: Replace phone use with activities that bring you joy, like reading, exercising, or spending time with loved ones.

5. **Practice Mindfulness**: Be aware of when and why you're reaching for your phone. Ask yourself, *Is this really necessary?*

Phone dependence is a tough habit to break, but it's not impossible. By recognizing the everyday habits that signal dependence, you can start to take back control of your time and attention. Remember, your phone is a tool—not a trap. You've got this.

◆ Assessing Your Relationship with Your Phone (Quiz)

- Let's get real for a moment. How often do you stop and think about your relationship with your phone? For most of us, it's just there—always in our hands, always in our pockets, always within reach. But have you ever wondered if your phone is helping you or holding you back? The truth is, many of us are more dependent on our phones than we realize. And the first step to breaking free from that dependence is understanding where you stand.

- That's where this quiz comes in. It's designed to help you assess your relationship with your phone. Are you in control, or is your phone controlling you? Let's find out.

How to Take the Quiz

- This quiz is simple. Just answer each question honestly, and keep track of your answers. At the end, we'll tally up your score and help you understand what it means. Remember, this isn't about judging yourself—it's about gaining awareness so you can make positive changes.

The Quiz

1. How often do you check your phone?

- A) Only when I get a call or text.

- B) A few times an hour.

- C) Constantly—I'm always scrolling or checking something.

2. How do you feel when you don't have your phone?

- A) Totally fine. I don't even notice it's gone.

- B) A little uneasy, but I can manage.

- C) Anxious or stressed. I feel like I'm missing something important.

3. Do you use your phone during meals?

- A) Never. Meals are for eating and talking.

- B) Sometimes, if I'm alone or waiting for someone.

- C) Always. I can't eat without scrolling.

4. How do you start your day?

- A) I wake up and focus on my morning routine—no phone.

- B) I check my phone briefly for messages or the news.

- C) The first thing I do is grab my phone and start scrolling.

5. How do you handle boredom?

- A) I find something productive or relaxing to do—no phone needed.

- B) I might check my phone for a few minutes.

- C) I immediately reach for my phone and start scrolling or playing games.

6. How often do you lose track of time on your phone?

- A) Rarely. I use my phone intentionally and don't get sucked in.

- B) Sometimes, especially on social media.

- C) All the time. I'll look up and realize hours have gone by.

7. Do you use your phone in social situations?

- A) Never. I focus on the people I'm with.

- B) Sometimes, if the conversation lags.

- C) All the time. I'm often scrolling while talking to others.

8. How do you feel about notifications?

- A) I keep them off. I check my phone when I want to.

- B) I get a few notifications, but they don't bother me.

- C) I can't ignore them. I have to check every alert right away.

9. How does your phone affect your sleep?

- A) I don't use my phone before bed, so it doesn't affect my sleep.

- B) I use it a little before bed, but it doesn't keep me up.

- C) I'm on my phone right up until I fall asleep, and it often keeps me awake.

10. How much time do you spend on your phone each day?

- A) Less than an hour. I use it only when necessary.

- B) A few hours. I use it for work and leisure.

- C) More than 5 hours. I'm on it all the time.

Scoring Your Quiz

- Now that you've answered the questions, let's tally up your score. Give yourself:

L.Harris Spike

- **1 point** for every A answer.

- **2 points** for every B answer.

- **3 points** for every C answer.

- Add up your points and see where you fall:

- **10–15 points**: You're in control. Your relationship with your phone is healthy and balanced.

- **16–25 points**: You're slipping into dependence. Your phone is starting to take up more of your time and attention than it should.

- **26–30 points**: Your phone is running the show. It's time to take a step back and reassess your relationship with your device.

What Your Score Means

If You Scored 10–15 Points: You're in Control

- Congratulations! You have a healthy relationship with your phone. You use it as a tool when you need it, but it doesn't control your life. You're able to put it down and focus on the people and activities that matter most. Keep up the good work, and remember to stay mindful of your habits as technology continues to evolve.

If You Scored 16–25 Points: You're Slipping into Dependence

- You're not fully addicted to your phone, but it's starting to take up more of your time and attention than it should. You might find yourself reaching for your phone out of habit, even when you don't really need to. The good news is, you're aware of the issue, and that's the first step to making a change. Consider setting some boundaries, like turning off notifications or designating phone-free times during your day.

If You Scored 26–30 Points: Your Phone Is Running the Show

- It's time to face the facts: your phone is controlling your life. You're spending hours each day scrolling, checking, and tapping, and it's taking a toll on your mental health, relationships, and productivity. But don't despair—you're not alone, and there's always a way to break free. Start by setting small, achievable goals, like reducing your screen time by 30 minutes a day or leaving your phone in another room during meals. Over time, these small changes can add up to big results.

Key Stats at a Glance

Quiz Insights	Details
Average daily phone use	7 hours/day (DataReportal, 2023)

Anxiety without phone	71% feel anxious when separated from their phone (BankMyCell, 2021)
Phone use during meals	51% use phones during meals (Pew Research, 2021)
Sleep disruption	90% use phones before bed; 60% report poor sleep (National Sleep Foundation)
Time lost to scrolling	Average person spends 2.5 hours/day on social media (DataReportal, 2023)

Next Steps

- No matter where you scored, there's always room for improvement. Here are a few tips to help you take the next step toward a healthier relationship with your phone:

1. **Set Boundaries**: Decide when and where you'll use your phone. For example, no phones during meals or after 8 p.m.

2. **Turn Off Notifications**: Only allow essential notifications (like calls and texts) to come through.

3. **Create Phone-Free Zones**: Designate certain areas, like your bedroom or dining room, as phone-free zones.

4. **Find Alternatives**: Replace phone use with activities that bring you joy, like reading, exercising, or spending time with loved ones.

5. **Practice Mindfulness**: Be aware of when and why you're reaching for your phone. Ask yourself, *Is this really necessary?*

- This quiz is just the beginning. By understanding your relationship with your phone, you can start to make changes that will improve your mental health, relationships, and overall well-being.

◆ Emotional and Social Impacts

Let's talk about something that doesn't get enough attention: how our phones affect our emotions and relationships. Sure, we know that spending too much time on our phones can waste time, but what about the deeper costs? The truth is, our phones don't just steal our time—they can also mess with our emotions, our mental health, and even our relationships with the people we care about most. And the worst part? We often don't even realize it's happening until it's too late.

So, let's take a closer look at the emotional and social impacts of phone addiction. If you've ever felt lonely, anxious, or disconnected, even when surrounded by people, your phone might be part of the problem.

1. The Emotional Rollercoaster

Our phones are designed to keep us hooked, and one of the ways they do that is by playing with our emotions. Every time you get a like, a comment, or a new message, your brain gets a little hit of dopamine—the "feel-good" chemical. This makes you feel happy, even if just for a moment. But here's the catch: that happiness doesn't last. As soon as the dopamine wears off, you're left wanting more.

This constant cycle of highs and lows can take a toll on your emotional well-being. A 2022 study by the *Journal of Social and Clinical Psychology* found that people who spent more than **2 hours a day** on social media were **three times more likely** to feel depressed or anxious. Why? Because social media often makes us feel like we're not good enough. We compare our lives to the highlight reels of others, and it leaves us feeling empty.

2. The Loneliness Trap

Here's the irony: our phones are supposed to connect us, but they can actually make us feel more alone. A 2021 survey by *Cigna* found that **61% of adults** in the U.S. reported feeling lonely. And guess what? Heavy phone users were more likely to feel this way.

Why does this happen? Because online interactions can't replace real-life connections. Sure, you might have hundreds of friends on Facebook or followers on Instagram, but how many of those relationships are meaningful? When we spend too much time online, we miss out on the deep, face-to-face connections that truly make us feel loved and supported.

3. The Comparison Game

One of the biggest emotional pitfalls of phone addiction is the constant comparison. Social media is full of people posting their best moments—perfect vacations, flawless selfies, and endless achievements. But here's the thing: what you see online isn't the full picture. It's a curated version of reality, designed to make people look their best.

When we compare our everyday lives to these highlight reels, it's easy to feel like we're falling short. A 2020 study by the *University of Pennsylvania* found that people who spent less time on social media reported feeling **significantly happier** and more satisfied with their lives. Why? Because they weren't constantly comparing themselves to others.

4. The Impact on Relationships

Our phones don't just affect how we feel—they also affect how we connect with others. Have you ever been in a conversation with someone, only to realize they're half-listening because they're scrolling through their phone? This behavior, known as **phubbing** (phone snubbing), can damage even the strongest relationships.

A 2021 survey by *Pew Research Center* found that **51% of people** said their partner was distracted by their phone during conversations. And it's not just romantic relationships that suffer. Parents who are glued to their phones may miss out on meaningful moments with their children. A study published in *Child Development* found that kids whose parents were frequently on their phones felt less important and more disconnected.

5. The Stress of Constant Connectivity

Our phones make it easy to stay connected 24/7, but this constant connectivity can be a major source of stress. Every time your phone buzzes with a notification, your brain releases a small amount of cortisol—the stress hormone. Over time, this constant state of alertness can lead to chronic stress, which has been linked to a host of health problems, including heart disease and weakened immune systems.

A 2022 study by *Harvard University* found that people who checked their phones frequently throughout the day reported higher levels of stress and anxiety. The solution? Setting boundaries. Turning off non-essential notifications and designating phone-free times can help you reclaim your peace of mind.

6. The Loss of Presence

Perhaps the most heartbreaking impact of phone addiction is the loss of presence. When we're glued to our screens, we're not fully present in our own lives. We miss the little things—the sound of laughter, the beauty of a sunset, or the joy of a spontaneous conversation. These moments may seem small, but they're the ones that make life meaningful. And once they're gone, we can't get them back.

A 2021 survey by *BankMyCell* found that **71% of people** felt their phones distracted them from being present in their daily lives. Whether it's during a family dinner, a walk in nature, or a quiet moment alone, our phones often pull us away from the experiences that truly matter.

Key Stats at a Glance

Emotional and Social Impacts	Details
Depression and anxiety	>2 hours/day on social media = 3x higher risk (Journal of Psychology, 2022)
Loneliness	61% of adults feel lonely; heavy phone users more likely (Cigna, 2021)
Comparison and happiness	Less social media use = higher life satisfaction (University of Penn, 2020)

Phubbing	51% say their partner is distracted by their phone (Pew Research, 2021)
Stress from notifications	Frequent phone checks linked to higher stress (Harvard, 2022)
Loss of presence	71% feel phones distract them from being present (BankMyCell, 2021)

What Can You Do?

If you've recognized some of these emotional and social impacts in your own life, don't worry—you're not alone, and there's always a way to make a change. Here are a few tips to help you get started:

1. **Set Boundaries**: Decide when and where you'll use your phone. For example, no phones during meals or after 8 p.m.

2. **Turn Off Notifications**: Only allow essential notifications (like calls and texts) to come through.

3. **Practice Mindfulness**: Be aware of when and why you're reaching for your phone. Ask yourself, *Is this really necessary?*

4. **Prioritize Real-Life Connections**: Spend more time with people in person, not just online.

5. **Take Regular Breaks**: Schedule phone-free times during your day, like during meals or before bed.

1.3 The High Price of Always Being Connected

◆ Mental Health Consequences

Let's talk about something that's often overlooked when we discuss phone addiction: its impact on mental health. We know that spending too much time on our phones can waste time and distract us, but what about the deeper effects? The truth is, our phones don't just steal our attention—they can also take a toll on our mental well-being. From anxiety and depression to sleep problems and stress, the mental health consequences of phone addiction are real, and they're affecting more of us than we realize.

If you've ever felt overwhelmed, anxious, or just "off" after spending too much time on your phone, you're not alone. Let's dive into the ways phone addiction can mess with your mental health—and what you can do about it.

1. Anxiety: The Constant State of Alert

Our phones are designed to keep us hooked, and one of the ways they do that is by keeping us in a constant state of alert. Every time your phone buzzes with a notification, your brain releases a small amount of cortisol—the stress hormone. Over time, this constant state of alertness can lead to chronic anxiety.

A 2022 study by *Harvard University* found that people who checked their phones frequently throughout the day reported higher levels of anxiety. Why? Because our brains aren't built to handle the constant stream of information, notifications, and updates that our phones deliver. It's like being in a never-ending state of "fight or flight," and it can leave you feeling exhausted and on edge.

2. Depression: The Comparison Trap

Social media is one of the biggest culprits when it comes to phone addiction and mental health. Platforms like Instagram, Facebook, and TikTok are full of people posting their best moments—perfect vacations, flawless selfies, and endless achievements. But here's the thing: what you see online isn't the full picture. It's a curated version of reality, designed to make people look their best.

When we compare our everyday lives to these highlight reels, it's easy to feel like we're falling short. A 2022 study by the *Journal of Social and Clinical Psychology* found that people who spent more than **2 hours a day** on social media were **three times more likely** to feel depressed. Why? Because constant comparison can lead to feelings of inadequacy, low self-esteem, and even hopelessness.

3. Sleep Problems: The Blue Light Effect

Our phones don't just affect our mental health during the day— they can also mess with our sleep. The blue light emitted by our phones interferes with the production of melatonin, the hormone that helps us sleep. A 2021 study by the *National Sleep Foundation* found that **90% of people** use their phones within an hour of bedtime, and **60%** say it affects their sleep quality.

Poor sleep doesn't just leave you feeling tired—it can also worsen mental health issues like anxiety and depression. When we don't get enough rest, our brains struggle to regulate emotions, making us more prone to mood swings and irritability.

4. Stress: The Pressure to Be Always On

Our phones make it easy to stay connected 24/7, but this constant connectivity can be a major source of stress. Whether it's work emails, group chats, or social media updates, there's always something demanding our attention. A 2021 survey by *Deloitte* found that **60% of people** felt stressed by the pressure to always be available on their phones.

This constant pressure can lead to burnout, a state of emotional, physical, and mental exhaustion. When we're always "on," we don't give ourselves time to rest and recharge, which can take a serious toll on our mental health.

5. Loneliness: The Illusion of Connection

Here's the irony: our phones are supposed to connect us, but they can actually make us feel more alone. A 2021 survey by *Cigna* found that **61% of adults** in the U.S. reported feeling lonely. And guess what? Heavy phone users were more likely to feel this way.

Why does this happen? Because online interactions can't replace real-life connections. Sure, you might have hundreds of friends on Facebook or followers on Instagram, but how many of those relationships are meaningful? When we spend too much time online, we miss out on the deep, face-to-face connections that truly make us feel loved and supported.

6. Attention Problems: The Fragmented Mind

Our phones are designed to distract us, and they're really good at it. Every time we get a notification, our focus is pulled away from what we're doing. Research from the *University of California, Irvine* found that it takes an average of **23 minutes** to get back on track after a distraction. That means every time you check your phone, you're losing almost half an hour of productive time.

Over time, this constant switching between tasks can make it harder to concentrate and stay focused. It can also lead to feelings of overwhelm and frustration, as we struggle to keep up with the demands of our daily lives.

Key Stats at a Glance

Mental Health Consequences	Details

Anxiety	Frequent phone checks linked to higher anxiety (Harvard, 2022)
Depression	>2 hours/day on social media = 3x higher risk (Journal of Psychology, 2022)
Sleep problems	90% use phones before bed; 60% report poor sleep (National Sleep Foundation)
Stress	60% feel stressed by constant connectivity (Deloitte, 2021)
Loneliness	61% of adults feel lonely; heavy phone users more likely (Cigna, 2021)
Attention problems	23 minutes to refocus after a distraction (University of California, 2018)

What Can You Do?

If you've recognized some of these mental health consequences in your own life, don't worry—you're not alone, and there's always a way to make a change. Here are a few tips to help you get started:

1. **Set Boundaries**: Decide when and where you'll use your phone. For example, no phones during meals or after 8 p.m.

2. **Turn Off Notifications**: Only allow essential notifications (like calls and texts) to come through.

3. **Practice Mindfulness**: Be aware of when and why you're reaching for your phone. Ask yourself, *Is this really necessary?*

4. **Prioritize Sleep**: Create a bedtime routine that doesn't involve your phone. Try reading a book or meditating instead.

5. **Take Regular Breaks**: Schedule phone-free times during your day, like during meals or before bed.

◆ Productivity and Creativity Loss

Let's talk about something that might hit close to home: how your phone is sabotaging your productivity and creativity. You might think that your phone helps you get things done—after all, it's a tool for communication, organization, and even inspiration. But the truth is, your phone is probably doing more harm than good when it comes to getting things done and thinking creatively. From constant distractions to the endless pull of social media, our phones are designed to keep us hooked—and that comes at a cost.

If you've ever sat down to work on a project, only to find yourself scrolling through Instagram or checking emails for hours, you're not alone. Let's break down how phone addiction is killing your productivity and creativity—and what you can do to take back control.

1. The Distraction Problem

Our phones are distraction machines. Every time you get a notification—whether it's a text, an email, or a social media update—your focus is pulled away from what you're doing. And here's the kicker: it takes time to get back on track. Research from the *University of California, Irvine* found that it takes an average of **23 minutes** to refocus after a distraction. That means every time you check your phone, you're losing almost half an hour of productive time.

A 2021 study by *Dscout* found that the average person touches their phone **2,617 times a day**. That's a lot of interruptions! And each one chips away at your ability to concentrate and get things done. Over time, these distractions add up, leaving you feeling overwhelmed and unproductive.

2. The Myth of Multitasking

Many of us like to think we're good at multitasking, but the truth is, our brains aren't built for it. When we try to do multiple things at once—like answering a text while working on a report—we're not actually multitasking. We're just switching rapidly between tasks, and that comes at a cost.

A 2018 study by *Stanford University* found that people who multitask with their phones are **40% less productive** than those who focus on one task at a time. Why? Because every time you switch tasks, your brain has to reset, which takes time and mental energy. The result? You end up working harder but accomplishing less.

3. The Creativity Killer

Creativity thrives in moments of quiet and focus. It's when we let our minds wander that we come up with our best ideas. But our phones are constantly pulling us out of that creative zone. Every time you check your phone, you're interrupting your flow and stifling your creativity.

A 2020 study by the *University of London* found that people who spent more time on their phones were less likely to engage in creative activities like writing, drawing, or problem-solving. Why? Because constant phone use keeps our brains in a state of shallow thinking, making it harder to dive deep and come up with innovative ideas.

4. The Procrastination Trap

Let's be honest: our phones are a great way to procrastinate. When we're faced with a difficult task, it's easy to reach for our phones and distract ourselves with something easier or more enjoyable. But here's the problem: procrastination doesn't just waste time—it also increases stress and makes it harder to get started.

A 2022 survey by *RescueTime* found that **75% of people** admitted to using their phones to procrastinate at work. And the more we procrastinate, the more overwhelmed we feel, creating a vicious cycle of stress and inaction.

5. The Impact on Deep Work

Deep work—the ability to focus intensely on a task without distractions—is essential for productivity and creativity. But our phones make deep work almost impossible. Every notification, every buzz, every urge to check your phone pulls you out of that focused state.

A 2021 study by *Microsoft* found that the average person loses **31 hours a month** to phone distractions. That's almost a full workweek! And when we're constantly interrupted, we never get the chance to dive deep and do our best work.

6. The Social Media Time Sink

Social media is one of the biggest culprits when it comes to productivity loss. Platforms like Instagram, Facebook, and TikTok are designed to keep you scrolling, and they're really good at it. A 2023 report by *DataReportal* found that the average person spends **2.5 hours a day** on social media. That's **17.5**

hours a week—time that could be spent on more productive or creative pursuits.

And it's not just the time spent scrolling that's the problem. Social media also affects our ability to focus. A 2022 study by the *University of Pennsylvania* found that people who spent less time on social media reported higher levels of focus and productivity.

Key Stats at a Glance

Productivity and Creativity Loss	Details
Time lost to distractions	23 minutes to refocus after a distraction (University of California, 2018)
Multitasking impact	40% less productive when multitasking (Stanford, 2018)
Creativity loss	Less creative engagement with high phone use (University of London, 2020)
Procrastination	75% use phones to procrastinate at work (RescueTime, 2022)

Deep work interruptions	31 hours/month lost to phone distractions (Microsoft, 2021)
Social media time sink	2.5 hours/day spent on social media (DataReportal, 2023)

What Can You Do?

If you've recognized some of these productivity and creativity killers in your own life, don't worry—you're not alone, and there's always a way to make a change. Here are a few tips to help you get started:

1. **Set Boundaries**: Decide when and where you'll use your phone. For example, no phones during work hours or creative sessions.

2. **Turn Off Notifications**: Only allow essential notifications (like calls and texts) to come through.

3. **Use Focus Tools**: Apps like Forest or Freedom can help you stay focused by blocking distracting apps and websites.

4. **Schedule Deep Work Time**: Set aside specific times during the day for deep, focused work. Turn off your phone or put it in another room.

5. **Take Regular Breaks**: Use techniques like the Pomodoro Method to work in focused bursts, with short breaks in between.

◆ Strained Relationships and Missed Moments

Let's talk about something that's easy to overlook but incredibly important: how our phones affect our relationships and the moments we share with the people we care about. You might think that your phone helps you stay connected, but the truth is, it can often do the opposite. From strained relationships to missed moments, our phones can create distance between us and the people who matter most—even when we're sitting right next to them.

If you've ever been in a conversation with someone who was more interested in their phone than in you, you know how frustrating it can feel. Or maybe you've been the one scrolling through your phone, only to realize later that you missed an important moment. Let's dive into how phone addiction is hurting our relationships and what we can do to fix it.

1. The Rise of Phubbing

Have you ever been talking to someone, only to have them pick up their phone and start scrolling mid-conversation? This behavior is so common that it has a name: **phubbing** (short for "phone snubbing"). And it's a major problem in relationships.

A 2021 survey by *Pew Research Center* found that **51% of people** said their partner was distracted by their phone during conversations. And it's not just romantic relationships that suffer. Friends, family members, and even coworkers can feel ignored or unimportant when we prioritize our phones over them.

Phubbing might seem harmless, but it can have serious consequences. A 2020 study by *Baylor University* found that phubbing can lead to lower relationship satisfaction, increased feelings of loneliness, and even conflicts between partners. When we're constantly checking our phones, we're sending a message that the person in front of us isn't as important as whatever's on our screen.

2. Missed Moments

Our phones don't just strain our relationships—they also cause us to miss out on important moments. Think about the last time you were at a family dinner, a friend's birthday party, or even just hanging out with your kids. Were you fully present, or were you half-listening while scrolling through your phone?

A 2021 survey by *BankMyCell* found that **71% of people** felt their phones distracted them from being present in their daily lives. Whether it's a child's first steps, a heartfelt conversation with a friend, or a beautiful sunset, these moments are precious—and once they're gone, we can't get them back.

3. The Impact on Kids

If you're a parent, your phone use doesn't just affect you—it also affects your kids. A study published in *Child Development* found that children whose parents were frequently on their phones felt less important and more disconnected. Kids need our attention and presence to feel loved and secure, and when we're glued to our screens, we're not giving them what they need.

The same study found that parents who spent more time on their phones were more likely to have conflicts with their children. Whether it's a missed homework assignment or a forgotten soccer game, these small moments of distraction can add up, creating tension and resentment over time.

4. The Illusion of Connection

Here's the irony: our phones are supposed to connect us, but they can actually make us feel more alone. A 2021 survey by *Cigna* found that **61% of adults** in the U.S. reported feeling lonely. And guess what? Heavy phone users were more likely to feel this way.

Why does this happen? Because online interactions can't replace real-life connections. Sure, you might have hundreds of friends on Facebook or followers on Instagram, but how many of those relationships are meaningful? When we spend too much time online, we miss out on the deep, face-to-face connections that truly make us feel loved and supported.

5. The Stress of Constant Connectivity

Our phones make it easy to stay connected 24/7, but this constant connectivity can be a major source of stress. Whether it's work emails, group chats, or social media updates, there's always something demanding our attention. A 2021 survey by *Deloitte* found that **60% of people** felt stressed by the pressure to always be available on their phones.

This constant pressure can lead to burnout, a state of emotional, physical, and mental exhaustion. When we're always "on," we don't give ourselves time to rest and recharge, which can take a serious toll on our relationships. We're more likely to snap at our loved ones, miss important moments, and feel disconnected from the people around us.

6. The Loss of Presence

Perhaps the most heartbreaking impact of phone addiction is the loss of presence. When we're glued to our screens, we're not fully present in our own lives. We miss the little things—the sound of laughter, the beauty of a sunset, or the joy of a spontaneous conversation. These moments may seem small, but they're the ones that make life meaningful. And once they're gone, we can't get them back.

A 2021 survey by *BankMyCell* found that **71% of people** felt their phones distracted them from being present in their daily lives. Whether it's during a family dinner, a walk in nature, or a quiet moment alone, our phones often pull us away from the experiences that truly matter.

Key Stats at a Glance

Strained Relationships and Missed Moments	Details
Phubbing	51% say their partner is distracted by their phone (Pew Research, 2021)
Missed moments	71% feel phones distract them from being present (BankMyCell, 2021)
Impact on kids	Kids feel less important when parents are on phones (Child Development)
Loneliness	61% of adults feel lonely; heavy phone users more likely (Cigna, 2021)
Stress from constant connectivity	60% feel stressed by always being available (Deloitte, 2021)

Loss of presence	71% feel phones distract them from being present (BankMyCell, 2021)

What Can You Do?

If you've recognized some of these issues in your own life, don't worry—you're not alone, and there's always a way to make a change. Here are a few tips to help you get started:

1. **Set Boundaries**: Decide when and where you'll use your phone. For example, no phones during meals or family time.

2. **Turn Off Notifications**: Only allow essential notifications (like calls and texts) to come through.

3. **Practice Mindfulness**: Be aware of when and why you're reaching for your phone. Ask yourself, *Is this really necessary?*

4. **Prioritize Real-Life Connections**: Spend more time with people in person, not just online.

5. **Take Regular Breaks**: Schedule phone-free times during your day, like during meals or before bed.

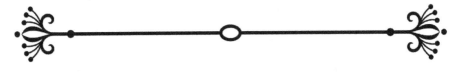

L.Harris Spike

Chapter 2: The Breakup Plan

2.1 Preparing for the Split

◆ Setting Your Intention: Why Do You Want to Quit?

Let's start with a simple question: *Why do you want to quit your phone addiction?* It might seem like an easy question, but the answer is more important than you think. Setting your intention—your reason for wanting to break free from your phone—is the first step toward creating real, lasting change. Without a clear "why," it's easy to fall back into old habits. But when you know exactly why you want to quit, you'll have the motivation and focus to stick with it, even when it gets tough.

So, let's dig deep. Why do you want to quit? What's driving you to make this change? Whether it's to improve your mental health, strengthen your relationships, or simply reclaim your time, your intention is your anchor. Let's explore some common reasons people want to break free from phone addiction—and how you can find your own "why."

1. To Improve Your Mental Health

One of the biggest reasons people want to quit phone addiction is to improve their mental health. Let's face it: our phones can be a major source of stress, anxiety, and even depression. From the constant notifications to the endless scroll of social media, our phones keep us in a state of constant alertness, making it hard to relax and unwind.

A 2022 study by the *Journal of Social and Clinical Psychology* found that people who spent more than **2 hours a day** on social media were **three times more likely** to feel depressed or anxious. If you've ever felt overwhelmed, stressed, or just "off" after spending too much time on your phone, you're not alone. Breaking free from phone addiction can help you reclaim your peace of mind and improve your overall mental well-being.

2. To Strengthen Your Relationships

Our phones are supposed to connect us, but they can often do the opposite. Have you ever been in a conversation with someone, only to realize they're more interested in their phone than in you? This behavior, known as **phubbing** (phone snubbing), can damage even the strongest relationships.

A 2021 survey by *Pew Research Center* found that **51% of people** said their partner was distracted by their phone during conversations. And it's not just romantic relationships that suffer. Friends, family members, and even coworkers can feel ignored or unimportant when we prioritize our phones over them.

If you want to strengthen your relationships and be more present with the people you care about, breaking free from phone addiction is a great place to start. By setting boundaries with your phone, you can show the people in your life that they matter—and create deeper, more meaningful connections.

3. To Reclaim Your Time

Let's be honest: our phones are a huge time suck. A 2023 report by *DataReportal* found that the average person spends **7 hours a day** on their phone. That's almost half of your waking hours! And when you add it all up, that's over **2,500 hours a year** spent scrolling, swiping, and tapping.

If you've ever felt like there aren't enough hours in the day, your phone might be part of the problem. Breaking free from phone addiction can help you reclaim your time and focus on the things that truly matter—whether it's spending time with loved ones, pursuing a hobby, or simply enjoying some quiet time alone.

4. To Boost Your Productivity

Our phones are designed to distract us, and they're really good at it. Every time you get a notification, your focus is pulled away from what you're doing. Research from the *University of California, Irvine* found that it takes an average of **23 minutes** to get back on track after a distraction. That means every time you check your phone, you're losing almost half an hour of productive time.

If you've ever struggled to stay focused at work or felt like you're not getting enough done, your phone might be to blame. Breaking free from phone addiction can help you boost your productivity and get more done in less time. By setting boundaries with your phone, you can create a more focused, efficient work environment—and have more time for the things you love.

5. To Rediscover Your Creativity

Creativity thrives in moments of quiet and focus. It's when we let our minds wander that we come up with our best ideas. But our phones are constantly pulling us out of that creative zone. Every time you check your phone, you're interrupting your flow and stifling your creativity.

A 2020 study by the *University of London* found that people who spent more time on their phones were less likely to engage in creative activities like writing, drawing, or problem-solving. If you've ever felt stuck or uninspired, breaking free from phone addiction can help you rediscover your creativity and tap into your full potential.

6. To Be More Present

Perhaps the most important reason to quit phone addiction is to be more present in your own life. When we're glued to our screens, we're not fully present in the moment. We miss the little things—the sound of laughter, the beauty of a sunset, or the joy of a spontaneous conversation. These moments may seem small, but they're the ones that make life meaningful.

A 2021 survey by *BankMyCell* found that **71% of people** felt their phones distracted them from being present in their daily lives. If you want to live a more mindful, present life, breaking free from phone addiction is a great place to start. By setting boundaries with your phone, you can create more space for the moments that truly matter.

Key Stats at a Glance

Reasons to Quit Phone Addiction	Details
Mental health improvement	>2 hours/day on social media = 3x higher risk of depression (Psychology)
Relationship strengthening	51% say their partner is distracted by their phone (Pew Research, 2021)
Time reclamation	Average person spends 7 hours/day on their phone (DataReportal, 2023)
Productivity boost	23 minutes to refocus after a distraction (University of California, 2018)

Creativity rediscovery	Less creative engagement with high phone use (University of London, 2020)
Presence	71% feel phones distract them from being present (BankMyCell, 2021)

How to Set Your Intention

Now that you've explored some common reasons to quit phone addiction, it's time to set your own intention. Here's how to get started:

1. **Reflect on Your "Why"**: Take some time to think about why you want to quit. What's driving you to make this change? Write it down and keep it somewhere visible, like on your fridge or in your journal.

2. **Be Specific**: The more specific your intention, the better. Instead of saying, "I want to use my phone less," try something like, "I want to spend more quality time with my family without distractions."

3. **Visualize Success**: Imagine what your life will look like once you've broken free from phone addiction. How will you feel? What will you do with your extra time and energy? Visualizing your success can help you stay motivated.

4. **Start Small**: Breaking free from phone addiction doesn't have to happen overnight. Start with small, achievable goals, like turning off notifications or setting a daily screen time limit.

5. **Celebrate Progress**: Every step you take toward breaking free from phone addiction is worth celebrating. Whether it's going an hour without checking your phone or spending a whole day offline, take time to acknowledge your progress.

Your Intention Is Your Anchor

Setting your intention is the first step toward breaking free from phone addiction. It's your anchor, your motivation, and your guide. When you know why you want to quit, you'll have the focus and determination to stick with it, even when it gets tough.

So, what's your "why"? Whether it's to improve your mental health, strengthen your relationships, or simply reclaim your time, your intention is the key to creating a healthier, more balanced relationship with technology. You've got this

♦ Overcoming the Fear of Missing Out (FOMO)

Let's talk about something that keeps many of us glued to our phones: the **fear of missing out**, or FOMO. It's that nagging feeling that something exciting or important is happening somewhere else, and if you're not constantly checking your phone, you'll miss it. Whether it's a friend's party, a breaking news story, or just the latest viral meme, FOMO drives us to check our phones over and over again—even when we know we shouldn't.

But here's the thing: FOMO isn't just annoying—it's also exhausting. It keeps us in a constant state of anxiety, always wondering if we're missing out on something better. And the worst part? Most of the time, we're not missing anything important at all. So, how do we break free from FOMO and reclaim our peace of mind? Let's dive in.

What Is FOMO, and Why Does It Happen?

FOMO is the fear that you're missing out on something exciting or important. It's that feeling you get when you see your friends posting pictures from a party you weren't invited to, or when you hear about a big news story that everyone's talking about. FOMO is especially common on social media, where everyone's lives look perfect and exciting—even when they're not.

A 2022 survey by *BankMyCell* found that **69% of people** experience FOMO because of social media. Why? Because social media is designed to make us feel like we're missing out. Every time you scroll through your feed, you're bombarded with images of people having fun, achieving success, and living their best lives. It's easy to feel like your own life doesn't measure up.

The Impact of FOMO

FOMO might seem harmless, but it can have serious consequences for your mental health and well-being. Here's how:

1. **Anxiety and Stress**: FOMO keeps us in a constant state of alertness, always wondering if we're missing something important. This can lead to chronic anxiety and stress. A 2021 study by *Harvard University* found that people who experienced high levels of FOMO also reported higher levels of anxiety and stress.

2. **Lower Self-Esteem**: When we compare our lives to the highlight reels we see on social media, it's easy to feel like we're not good enough. A 2020 study by the *University of Pennsylvania* found that people who spent less time on social media reported higher levels of self-esteem and life satisfaction.

3. **Poor Sleep**: FOMO can also affect your sleep. If you're constantly checking your phone for updates, you're more likely to have trouble falling asleep and staying asleep. A 2021 study by the *National Sleep Foundation* found that **60% of people** who used their phones before bed reported poor sleep quality.

4. **Wasted Time**: FOMO drives us to check our phones constantly, even when there's no real reason to. A 2023 report by *DataReportal* found that the average person spends **2.5 hours a day** on social media. That's a lot of time that could be spent on more meaningful activities.

How to Overcome FOMO

Now that we know how FOMO affects us, let's talk about how to overcome it. Here are some practical steps you can take to break free from FOMO and reclaim your peace of mind:

1. Recognize That FOMO Is an Illusion

The first step to overcoming FOMO is recognizing that it's often based on an illusion. What you see on social media isn't the full picture—it's a curated version of reality. People post their best moments, not their everyday struggles. So, when you feel like you're missing out, remind yourself that what you're seeing isn't the whole story.

2. Set Boundaries with Your Phone

One of the best ways to overcome FOMO is to set boundaries with your phone. Here are a few tips:

- **Turn Off Notifications**: Only allow essential notifications (like calls and texts) to come through.

- **Set Specific Times for Checking Your Phone**: Instead of checking your phone constantly, set specific times during the day to catch up on social media or news.

- **Create Phone-Free Zones**: Designate certain areas, like your bedroom or dining room, as phone-free zones.

3. Practice Mindfulness

Mindfulness is the practice of being fully present in the moment. When you're mindful, you're less likely to get caught up in FOMO because you're focused on what's happening right now. Here are a few ways to practice mindfulness:

- **Take Deep Breaths**: When you feel the urge to check your phone, take a few deep breaths instead. This can help you calm down and refocus.

- **Engage Your Senses**: Pay attention to what's happening around you. What do you see, hear, smell, and feel? This can help you stay grounded in the present moment.

- **Limit Multitasking**: Focus on one thing at a time. When you're eating, just eat. When you're talking to someone, just talk. This can help you be more present and less distracted.

4. Focus on What You Have, Not What You're Missing

Instead of focusing on what you might be missing out on, focus on what you have. Take a moment to appreciate the people, experiences, and opportunities in your life. Gratitude can help shift your mindset from scarcity to abundance, making it easier to overcome FOMO.

5. Take a Break from Social Media

Sometimes, the best way to overcome FOMO is to take a break from social media altogether. A 2020 study by the *University of Pennsylvania* found that people who took a break from social media reported lower levels of FOMO and higher levels of well-being. Even a short break—like a day or a weekend—can help you reset and gain perspective.

Key Stats at a Glance

FOMO Insights	Details
FOMO prevalence	69% experience FOMO due to social media (BankMyCell, 2022)
Anxiety and stress	High FOMO linked to higher anxiety (Harvard, 2021)
Self-esteem	Less social media use = higher self-esteem (University of Penn, 2020)
Sleep disruption	60% report poor sleep due to phone use before bed (National Sleep Foundation)

Time spent on social media	Average person spends 2.5 hours/day on social media (DataReportal, 2023)

Real-Life Examples of Overcoming FOMO

Let's look at a few real-life examples of how people have overcome FOMO:

1. **Sarah's Story**: Sarah used to check her phone constantly, worried she'd miss out on something important. But after realizing how much time she was wasting, she decided to set boundaries. She turned off non-essential notifications and set specific times for checking her phone. Over time, she found that she was less anxious and more present in her daily life.

2. **Mike's Story**: Mike was always comparing himself to others on social media, which made him feel like he wasn't good enough. He decided to take a break from social media for a month. During that time, he focused on his hobbies and spent more time with friends and family. By the end of the month, he felt more confident and less worried about what others were doing.

3. **Emily's Story**: Emily used to feel like she had to say yes to every invitation, afraid she'd miss out on something fun. But after realizing how exhausted she was, she started saying no to things that didn't truly matter to her. She

found that she had more time for the things she loved—and she didn't feel like she was missing out at all.

Your Turn: Overcoming FOMO

Now it's your turn. What's one small step you can take today to overcome FOMO? Maybe it's turning off notifications, setting a time limit for social media, or simply taking a few deep breaths the next time you feel the urge to check your phone.

Identifying Your Phone Triggers

Let's get real for a moment. How many times have you told yourself, "I'll just check my phone for a minute," only to look up an hour later, wondering where the time went? If this sounds familiar, you're not alone. Many of us struggle with phone addiction, but the first step to breaking free is understanding what's driving it. And that starts with identifying your **phone triggers**.

Phone triggers are the situations, emotions, or habits that make you reach for your phone without even thinking about it. Maybe it's boredom, stress, or just the habit of scrolling before bed. Whatever it is, once you know your triggers, you can start to take control. So, let's dive in and figure out what's making you reach for your phone—and how to break the cycle.

What Are Phone Triggers?

Phone triggers are the things that make you want to check your phone. They can be external, like a notification or a specific time of day, or internal, like a feeling of boredom or anxiety. The key is to recognize these triggers so you can interrupt the habit and create healthier patterns.

For example, let's say you always check your phone when you're waiting in line. That's a trigger. Or maybe you reach for your phone when you're feeling stressed or overwhelmed. That's another trigger. Once you know what your triggers are, you can start to address them.

Common Phone Triggers

Here are some of the most common phone triggers—see if any of these sound familiar:

1. Notifications

Every time your phone buzzes or beeps, it's like a little tap on the shoulder, demanding your attention. A 2021 study by *Dscout* found that the average person gets **46 notifications a day**. That's a lot of interruptions! And each one is a potential trigger, pulling you back into the cycle of phone use.

2. Boredom

Boredom is one of the biggest triggers for phone use. When we're bored, our phones are an easy way to pass the time. A 2022 survey by *BankMyCell* found that **64% of people** said they used their phones to avoid boredom. But the problem is, this habit can quickly spiral out of control, leading to hours of mindless scrolling.

3. Stress and Anxiety

When we're feeling stressed or anxious, our phones can feel like a safe escape. Whether it's scrolling through social media, playing a game, or checking the news, our phones provide a temporary distraction from our problems. But here's the catch: this distraction doesn't solve the problem—it just delays it.

4. Social Situations

Have you ever been in a social situation where you felt awkward or uncomfortable, so you reached for your phone? This is a common trigger, especially for people who struggle with social anxiety. A 2021 survey by *Pew Research Center* found that **51% of people** said they used their phones to avoid awkward conversations.

5. Habitual Use

Sometimes, we reach for our phones simply out of habit. Maybe you always check your phone first thing in the morning, or maybe you scroll through social media before bed. These habits can be hard to break, but once you recognize them, you can start to create new, healthier routines.

How to Identify Your Triggers

Now that you know some common triggers, how do you figure out which ones apply to you? Here's a simple exercise to help you identify your phone triggers:

1. **Track Your Phone Use**: For the next few days, keep a log of when and why you use your phone. Write down the time, the situation, and how you were feeling. For example:

    o **Time**: 8:00 a.m.

    o **Situation**: Waiting for the bus

    o **Feeling**: Bored

2. **Look for Patterns**: After a few days, review your log and look for patterns. Are there certain times of day when you use your phone more? Certain situations or emotions that trigger phone use?

3. **Identify Your Triggers**: Based on your log, make a list of your top phone triggers. These are the situations, emotions, or habits that are driving your phone use.

Key Stats at a Glance

Common Phone Triggers	Details

Notifications	Average person gets 46 notifications/day (Dscout, 2021)
Boredom	64% use phones to avoid boredom (BankMyCell, 2022)
Stress and anxiety	Phones used as a distraction from stress (Psychology Today, 2021)
Social situations	51% use phones to avoid awkward conversations (Pew Research, 2021)
Habitual use	Many people check phones out of habit (Harvard, 2020)

How to Break the Cycle

Once you've identified your phone triggers, the next step is to break the cycle. Here are some practical tips to help you do that:

1. Turn Off Non-Essential Notifications

Notifications are one of the biggest triggers for phone use. To reduce their impact, turn off non-essential notifications. Only allow alerts that are truly important, like calls or texts. This will help you stay focused and reduce the urge to check your phone constantly.

2. Find Alternatives for Boredom

If boredom is a trigger for you, find other ways to pass the time. Instead of reaching for your phone, try reading a book, going for a walk, or doing a quick workout. These activities can help you break the habit of mindless scrolling and give you a sense of accomplishment.

3. Practice Stress-Relief Techniques

If stress or anxiety is a trigger, find healthier ways to cope. Instead of turning to your phone, try deep breathing, meditation, or journaling. These techniques can help you manage stress without relying on your phone as a distraction.

4. Be Present in Social Situations

If social situations are a trigger, try to be more present. Instead of reaching for your phone, focus on the conversation or the people around you. If you're feeling awkward, remind yourself that it's okay to feel uncomfortable—it's part of being human.

5. Create New Habits

If habitual use is a trigger, create new routines to replace the old ones. For example, instead of checking your phone first thing in the morning, try starting your day with a few minutes of stretching or meditation. Or, instead of scrolling before bed, try reading a book or listening to calming music.

Real-Life Examples of Breaking Triggers

Let's look at a few real-life examples of how people have identified and broken their phone triggers:

1. **Emma's Story**: Emma noticed that she always reached for her phone when she was bored at work. To break the habit, she started keeping a book at her desk. Whenever she felt the urge to check her phone, she would read a few pages instead. Over time, she found that she was more focused and less distracted.

2. **James's Story**: James realized that stress was a major trigger for his phone use. Whenever he felt overwhelmed, he would scroll through social media to escape. To break the cycle, he started practicing deep breathing exercises whenever he felt stressed. This helped him stay calm and focused, without relying on his phone.

3. **Sophia's Story**: Sophia noticed that she always checked her phone during social gatherings. To break the habit, she started leaving her phone in her bag during parties and dinners. This helped her be more present and enjoy the moment, without the distraction of her phone.

Your Turn: Identify and Break Your Triggers

Now it's your turn. Take a few days to track your phone use and identify your triggers. Once you know what's driving your phone addiction, you can start to take control. Remember, breaking free from phone addiction isn't about perfection—it's about progress.

Every small step you take brings you closer to a healthier relationship with technology.

2.2 Creating a Phone-Free Life

◆ Setting Boundaries: Screen Time Limits and No-Phone Zones

Let's face it: our phones are always there, always within reach, always demanding our attention. But what if we could take back control? What if we could set boundaries that help us use our phones less and live more? That's where **screen time limits** and **no-phone zones** come in. These simple but powerful tools can help you break free from phone addiction and create a healthier relationship with technology.

Setting boundaries isn't about cutting yourself off completely—it's about creating a balance. It's about deciding when, where, and how you use your phone, so it doesn't take over your life. So, let's dive into how you can set boundaries that work for you, whether it's limiting your screen time or creating spaces where your phone isn't allowed.

Why Set Boundaries?

Before we get into the how, let's talk about the why. Why is it so important to set boundaries with your phone? Here are a few reasons:

1. **Reclaim Your Time**: The average person spends 7 **hours a day** on their phone, according to a 2023 report by *DataReportal*. That's almost half of your waking hours! By setting boundaries, you can reclaim some of that time and use it for things that truly matter.

2. **Improve Your Mental Health**: Constant phone use can lead to stress, anxiety, and even depression. A 2022 study by the *Journal of Social and Clinical Psychology* found that people who spent more than **2 hours a day** on social media were **three times more likely** to feel depressed or anxious. Setting boundaries can help you reduce screen time and improve your mental well-being.

3. **Strengthen Your Relationships**: When you're constantly on your phone, it's hard to be fully present with the people around you. A 2021 survey by *Pew Research Center* found that **51% of people** said their partner was distracted by their phone during conversations. Setting boundaries can help you be more present and strengthen your relationships.

4. **Boost Your Productivity**: Our phones are designed to distract us, and that can take a toll on our productivity. Research from the *University of California, Irvine* found that it takes an average of **23 minutes** to refocus after a

distraction. By setting boundaries, you can reduce distractions and get more done.

How to Set Screen Time Limits

Screen time limits are one of the most effective ways to set boundaries with your phone. Here's how to do it:

1. Use Built-In Tools

Most smartphones have built-in tools to help you track and limit your screen time. For example:

- **iPhone**: Use the *Screen Time* feature to set daily limits for specific apps or categories (like social media or entertainment).

- **Android**: Use the *Digital Wellbeing* feature to set app timers and track your usage.

These tools can help you become more aware of how much time you're spending on your phone and set limits to reduce it.

2. Set Daily Limits

Start by setting a daily limit for your phone use. For example, you might decide to limit yourself to **2 hours a day** on social media or **1 hour a day** on entertainment apps. Be realistic—if you're currently spending 5 hours a day on your phone, cutting back to 1 hour might be too drastic. Start small and gradually reduce your limits over time.

3. Schedule Screen-Free Times

Another way to set screen time limits is to schedule specific times during the day when you won't use your phone. For example:

- **Morning**: Start your day without your phone. Use the first hour of your day for a morning routine, like exercise, meditation, or breakfast.

- **Meals**: Make meals a phone-free time. Focus on the food and the people you're with, not your screen.

- **Evening**: Wind down without your phone. Use the last hour before bed for relaxing activities, like reading or listening to music.

4. Use Apps to Help You

There are also apps that can help you set and stick to screen time limits. Some popular options include:

- **Forest**: This app helps you stay focused by planting a virtual tree that grows when you stay off your phone.

- **Freedom**: This app blocks distracting websites and apps for set periods of time.

- **StayFocusd**: This browser extension limits the amount of time you can spend on distracting websites.

How to Create No-Phone Zones

No-phone zones are areas where your phone isn't allowed. These spaces can help you be more present and reduce the temptation to check your phone constantly. Here's how to create them:

1. Bedroom

Your bedroom should be a place of rest and relaxation, not a place for scrolling through social media. A 2021 study by the *National Sleep Foundation* found that **90% of people** use their phones within an hour of bedtime, and **60%** say it affects their sleep quality. To create a no-phone zone in your bedroom:

- Charge your phone in another room overnight.
- Use an old-fashioned alarm clock instead of your phone.

2. Dining Room

Meals are a great time to connect with family and friends, but that's hard to do when everyone's on their phones. To create a no-phone zone in your dining room:

- Make a rule that phones aren't allowed at the table.
- Use a phone basket or box to collect phones before meals.

3. Workspace

If you work from home or have a home office, consider making it a no-phone zone. This can help you stay focused and productive. To create a no-phone zone in your workspace:

- Keep your phone in another room or in a drawer.

- Use a computer for work-related tasks instead of your phone.

4. Car

Using your phone while driving is not only dangerous—it's also illegal in many places. To create a no-phone zone in your car:

- Put your phone in the glove compartment or backseat.

- Use a hands-free device if you need to take a call.

Key Stats at a Glance

Setting Boundaries	Details
Average daily phone use	7 hours/day (DataReportal, 2023)
Mental health impact	>2 hours/day on social media = 3x higher risk of depression (Psychology)
Relationship strain	51% say their partner is distracted by their phone (Pew Research, 2021)
Productivity loss	23 minutes to refocus after a distraction (University of California, 2018)
Sleep disruption	90% use phones before bed; 60% report poor sleep (National Sleep Foundation)

Real-Life Examples of Setting Boundaries

Let's look at a few real-life examples of how people have set boundaries with their phones:

1. **Sarah's Story**: Sarah used to spend hours scrolling through social media every night before bed. To break the habit, she created a no-phone zone in her bedroom. She started charging her phone in the living room overnight and using an alarm clock instead. Over time, she found that she slept better and felt more rested in the morning.

2. **Mike's Story**: Mike noticed that he was constantly checking his phone during work, which made it hard to stay focused. To set boundaries, he started keeping his phone in a drawer during work hours. He also used the *Forest* app to stay focused and reduce distractions. As a result, he was able to get more done in less time.

3. **Emily's Story**: Emily realized that she was always on her phone during meals, which made it hard to connect with her family. To create a no-phone zone, she started using a phone basket at the dinner table. Everyone in the family would put their phones in the basket before eating. Over time, Emily found that meals became a time for meaningful conversations and connection.

Your Turn: Set Your Boundaries

Now it's your turn. What boundaries will you set with your phone? Maybe it's a daily screen time limit, a no-phone zone in your bedroom, or a rule that phones aren't allowed at the dinner table. Whatever it is, remember: setting boundaries isn't about cutting yourself off—it's about creating a healthier, more balanced relationship with technology.

◆ Alternative Habits to Fill the Void

Let's be honest: breaking free from phone addiction isn't just about cutting back on screen time—it's also about finding new ways to fill the time and energy that your phone used to take up. When you stop reaching for your phone every few minutes, you'll suddenly have a lot of free time on your hands. And if you don't have a plan for how to use that time, it's easy to fall back into old habits.

That's where **alternative habits** come in. These are activities that can replace the time you used to spend on your phone, helping you stay focused, productive, and fulfilled. Whether it's picking up a new hobby, spending more time with loved ones, or simply enjoying some quiet time alone, alternative habits can help you break free from phone addiction and create a more balanced life.

So, let's explore some alternative habits you can try—and how they can help you fill the void left by your phone.

Why Alternative Habits Matter

Before we dive into specific habits, let's talk about why they're so important. When you're used to spending hours on your phone every day, suddenly cutting back can leave a big hole in your routine. If you don't have something to replace that time, it's easy to feel bored, restless, or even anxious.

Alternative habits give you something positive to focus on, helping you break the cycle of phone addiction. They can also improve your mental health, boost your creativity, and strengthen your relationships. A 2021 study by the *University of London* found that people who engaged in hobbies and other offline activities reported higher levels of happiness and life satisfaction.

Alternative Habits to Try

Here are some alternative habits you can try to fill the void left by your phone:

1. Read a Book

Reading is a great way to relax, learn something new, and escape from the stresses of everyday life. Whether you prefer fiction, non-fiction, or poetry, reading can help you unwind and recharge. Plus, it's a much healthier way to pass the time than scrolling through social media.

- **Tip**: Keep a book with you at all times, so you can read whenever you have a spare moment—like waiting in line or riding the bus.

2. Get Moving

Exercise is one of the best ways to improve your physical and mental health. Whether it's going for a walk, hitting the gym, or trying a new sport, getting moving can help you feel more energized and focused. A 2022 study by the *American Psychological Association* found that regular exercise can reduce symptoms of anxiety and depression.

- **Tip**: Start small. Even a 10-minute walk can make a big difference.

3. Practice Mindfulness

Mindfulness is the practice of being fully present in the moment. It can help you reduce stress, improve your focus, and feel more connected to the world around you. There are many ways to practice mindfulness, from meditation to deep breathing to simply paying attention to your surroundings.

- **Tip**: Try a mindfulness app like *Headspace* or *Calm* to get started.

4. Spend Time with Loved Ones

When you're not glued to your phone, you'll have more time to connect with the people who matter most. Whether it's having a meaningful conversation, playing a game, or just hanging out, spending time with loved ones can help you feel more connected and supported.

- **Tip**: Schedule regular phone-free time with family and friends, like a weekly game night or dinner date.

5. Pick Up a New Hobby

Hobbies are a great way to fill your time and express your creativity. Whether it's painting, gardening, cooking, or playing an instrument, hobbies can help you relax, learn new skills, and feel a sense of accomplishment.

- **Tip**: Choose a hobby that you're genuinely interested in, and don't be afraid to try something new.

6. Journal

Journaling is a powerful way to process your thoughts and emotions. It can help you gain clarity, reduce stress, and track your progress as you work toward your goals. Plus, it's a great way to reflect on your day and celebrate your successes.

- **Tip**: Set aside a few minutes each day to write in your journal, whether it's in the morning, before bed, or during a break.

7. Get Outside

Spending time in nature can have a profound impact on your mental and physical health. Whether it's going for a hike, having a picnic, or just sitting in the park, getting outside can help you feel more relaxed and rejuvenated.

- **Tip**: Make it a goal to spend at least 30 minutes outside every day, even if it's just a walk around the block.

8. Volunteer

Volunteering is a great way to give back to your community and make a positive impact. Whether it's helping out at a local food bank, mentoring a young person, or cleaning up a park, volunteering can help you feel more connected and fulfilled.

- **Tip**: Choose a cause that you're passionate about, and start small. Even a few hours a month can make a big difference.

Key Stats at a Glance

Alternative Habits	Benefits
Reading	Reduces stress, improves focus, and boosts knowledge
Exercise	Reduces anxiety and depression, boosts energy
Mindfulness	Improves focus, reduces stress, and increases self-awareness

Spending time with loved ones	Strengthens relationships and increases feelings of connection
Hobbies	Boosts creativity, reduces stress, and provides a sense of accomplishment
Journaling	Helps process emotions, reduces stress, and tracks progress
Spending time in nature	Reduces stress, improves mood, and boosts physical health
Volunteering	Increases feelings of purpose and connection to community

Real-Life Examples of Alternative Habits

Let's look at a few real-life examples of how people have replaced phone time with alternative habits:

1. **Emma's Story**: Emma used to spend hours scrolling through social media every night before bed. To break the habit, she started reading instead. She set a goal to read one book a month and soon found that she was sleeping better and feeling more relaxed.

2. **James's Story**: James realized that he was always on his phone during his lunch break at work. To fill the time, he

started going for a walk instead. Not only did he feel more energized in the afternoons, but he also lost a few pounds.

3. **Sophia's Story**: Sophia used to spend hours on her phone every weekend, but she wanted to do something more meaningful with her time. She started volunteering at a local animal shelter and soon found that she looked forward to her weekends more than ever.

Your Turn: Find Your Alternative Habits

Now it's your turn. What alternative habits will you try to fill the void left by your phone? Maybe it's picking up a new hobby, spending more time with loved ones, or simply enjoying some quiet time alone. Whatever it is, remember: breaking free from phone addiction isn't about cutting yourself off—it's about creating a healthier, more balanced life.

◆ The Power of Digital Detox Days

Imagine this: a whole day without your phone. No notifications, no scrolling, no constant checking. Just you, the people around you, and the world as it is. Sounds refreshing, right? That's the power of a **digital detox day**. It's a chance to step away from the noise of technology and reconnect with yourself and the world around you.

Digital detox days are more than just a break from your phone— they're a reset for your mind, body, and soul. They give you the space to think, breathe, and be present in a way that's hard to do when you're constantly plugged in. And the best part? You don't have to give up your phone forever. Just one day can make a big difference.

So, let's dive into why digital detox days are so powerful, how to plan one, and what you can expect to gain from the experience.

Why Digital Detox Days Matter

Our phones are always there, always demanding our attention. Whether it's a notification, a text, or just the habit of checking, our phones keep us in a constant state of alertness. This can take a toll on our mental health, our relationships, and even our ability to think clearly.

A 2022 study by the *Journal of Social and Clinical Psychology* found that people who spent more than **2 hours a day** on social media were **three times more likely** to feel depressed or anxious. And it's not just mental health—our phones can also affect our sleep, our productivity, and our ability to connect with others.

Digital detox days give us a chance to step back from all of that. They help us break the cycle of constant connectivity and create space for the things that truly matter. Whether it's spending time with loved ones, enjoying nature, or simply being alone with your thoughts, a digital detox day can help you recharge and refocus.

How to Plan a Digital Detox Day

Planning a digital detox day doesn't have to be complicated. Here's a step-by-step guide to help you get started:

1. Choose a Day

The first step is to choose a day for your digital detox. It could be a weekend day when you don't have work or other commitments, or it could be a weekday if you can take some time off. The key is to choose a day when you can truly unplug and focus on yourself.

2. Set Boundaries

Once you've chosen a day, set some boundaries. Decide what "digital detox" means for you. For some people, it might mean no phone at all. For others, it might mean no social media or only using the phone for essential calls and texts. Whatever you decide, make sure you're clear on the rules before you start.

3. Plan Activities

One of the biggest challenges of a digital detox day is figuring out what to do with all that free time. To make the most of your day, plan some activities in advance. Here are a few ideas:

- **Spend time in nature**: Go for a hike, have a picnic, or just sit in the park.

- **Connect with loved ones**: Spend quality time with family and friends, without the distraction of phones.

- **Get creative**: Try a new hobby, like painting, writing, or cooking.

- **Practice mindfulness**: Meditate, do yoga, or simply sit quietly and reflect.

4. Prepare for Challenges

Let's be honest: going a whole day without your phone can be tough, especially if you're used to being constantly connected. To make it easier, prepare for the challenges ahead of time. For example:

- **Tell people in advance**: Let your family, friends, and coworkers know that you'll be offline for the day, so they don't worry.

- **Find alternatives**: If you usually use your phone for things like checking the time or listening to music, find alternatives, like a watch or a radio.

- **Stay busy**: Keep yourself occupied with activities, so you're less tempted to reach for your phone.

What to Expect from a Digital Detox Day

So, what can you expect from a digital detox day? Here are some of the benefits you might experience:

1. Improved Mental Health

One of the biggest benefits of a digital detox day is improved mental health. Without the constant buzz of notifications and the pressure to stay connected, you'll have a chance to relax and recharge. A 2021 study by the *University of Pennsylvania* found that people who took a break from social media reported lower levels of anxiety and depression.

2. Better Sleep

Our phones can interfere with our sleep in a number of ways, from the blue light they emit to the stress they cause. A digital detox day can help you break the cycle and get a better night's sleep. A 2021 study by the *National Sleep Foundation* found that people who used their phones less before bed reported better sleep quality.

3. Increased Productivity

When you're not constantly checking your phone, you'll have more time and energy to focus on the things that matter. Whether it's work, hobbies, or spending time with loved ones, a digital detox day can help you get more done and feel more accomplished.

4. Stronger Relationships

Without the distraction of phones, you'll have more opportunities to connect with the people around you. Whether it's having a meaningful conversation, playing a game, or just enjoying each other's company, a digital detox day can help you strengthen your relationships.

5. Greater Presence

Perhaps the most powerful benefit of a digital detox day is the sense of presence it brings. When you're not constantly plugged in, you'll have more opportunities to be fully present in the moment. Whether it's enjoying nature, savoring a meal, or simply being alone with your thoughts, a digital detox day can help you feel more connected to the world around you.

Key Stats at a Glance

Benefits of Digital Detox Days	Details
Improved mental health	Lower anxiety and depression (University of Pennsylvania, 2021)
Better sleep	Improved sleep quality (National Sleep Foundation, 2021)
Increased productivity	More focus and energy for meaningful activities
Stronger relationships	More meaningful connections with loved ones
Greater presence	Increased mindfulness and connection to the present moment

Real-Life Examples of Digital Detox Days

Let's look at a few real-life examples of how people have benefited from digital detox days:

1. **Sarah's Story**: Sarah used to spend hours on her phone every weekend, scrolling through social media and checking emails. To break the habit, she started taking digital detox days on Sundays. She would spend the day hiking, reading, and spending time with her family. Over time, she found that she felt more relaxed and refreshed on Monday mornings.

2. **Mike's Story**: Mike realized that he was always on his phone during family dinners, which made it hard to connect with his kids. To create more meaningful moments, he started taking digital detox days once a month. On those days, the whole family would leave their phones in a basket and spend the day playing games, cooking, and talking. Mike found that these days brought the family closer together.

3. **Emily's Story**: Emily used to feel overwhelmed by the constant demands of her phone, from work emails to social media notifications. To recharge, she started taking digital detox days every few months. She would spend the day in nature, hiking or sitting by the lake, and reflecting on her

goals and priorities. Emily found that these days helped her feel more focused and motivated.

2.3 The Tools for Success

♦ Apps to Help You Use Fewer Apps

It might sound a little ironic, but sometimes the best way to break free from phone addiction is to use your phone—just in a smarter way. There are apps out there designed to help you use fewer apps, stay focused, and take control of your screen time. These tools can help you set boundaries, track your usage, and even block distracting apps when you need to focus.

If you've ever felt like your phone is controlling you instead of the other way around, these apps can help you flip the script. Let's dive into some of the best apps to help you use fewer apps, and how they can help you create a healthier relationship with technology.

Why Use Apps to Reduce Phone Use?

Before we get into the specific apps, let's talk about why they're worth trying. Our phones are designed to keep us hooked. From endless scrolling to constant notifications, they're built to grab and hold our attention. But these apps are different. They're designed to help you take back control.

- ♦ A 2023 report by *DataReportal* found that the average person spends **7 hours a day** on their phone. That's almost half of your waking hours! And much of that time is spent on apps that don't add much value to your life—social media, games, and other distractions. By using apps that help you reduce your screen time, you can reclaim some of that time and use it for things that truly matter.

Top Apps to Help You Use Fewer Apps

Here are some of the best apps to help you reduce your phone use and stay focused:

1. Forest

What it does: Forest helps you stay focused by planting a virtual tree that grows when you stay off your phone. If you leave the app to check another app, your tree dies. Over time, you can grow a whole forest, which is a fun way to track your progress.

Why it works: Forest turns staying off your phone into a game. The visual reward of seeing your tree grow can motivate you to stay focused. Plus, the app partners with real tree-planting organizations, so your virtual trees can help plant real trees around the world.

Best for: People who need a little extra motivation to stay off their phones.

2. Freedom

What it does: Freedom lets you block distracting apps and websites for set periods of time. You can create custom blocklists, schedule focus sessions, and even sync your settings across multiple devices.

Why it works: Freedom takes the temptation out of the equation by blocking access to distracting apps altogether. It's like putting a lock on your phone's most addictive features.

Best for: People who struggle with self-control and need a hard barrier to stay focused.

3. StayFocusd

What it does: StayFocusd is a browser extension that limits the amount of time you can spend on distracting websites. Once you've used up your allotted time, the sites are blocked for the rest of the day.

Why it works: StayFocusd is great for people who spend too much time on websites like social media or news sites. It forces you to be mindful of how much time you're spending online.

Best for: People who do most of their phone use through a browser.

4. Screen Time (iOS) and Digital Wellbeing (Android)

What it does: These are built-in tools on your phone that track your screen time and app usage. You can set daily limits for specific apps, schedule downtime, and even set a bedtime mode to reduce distractions at night.

Why it works: Because these tools are built into your phone, they're easy to use and customize. They give you a clear picture of how much time you're spending on your phone and where you can cut back.

Best for: People who want a simple, built-in solution to track and reduce screen time.

5. Offtime

What it does: Offtime helps you disconnect by blocking distracting apps, filtering notifications, and even auto-responding to messages so you can focus without interruptions.

Why it works: Offtime is great for people who need to disconnect completely for a set period of time. It's perfect for work, family time, or just taking a break from your phone.

Best for: People who need to create strict boundaries around their phone use.

6. Moment

What it does: Moment tracks how much time you spend on your phone and which apps you use the most. It also offers coaching and challenges to help you reduce your screen time.

Why it works: Moment gives you a clear picture of your phone habits and provides actionable steps to help you cut back. The coaching feature is especially helpful for people who need guidance and support.

Best for: People who want to track their progress and get personalized tips to reduce screen time.

7. Flipd

What it does: Flipd lets you lock your phone for set periods of time, so you can focus on work, studying, or spending time with loved ones. You can also join focus groups and challenges to stay motivated.

Why it works: Flipd is great for people who need a little extra accountability. The focus groups and challenges make it feel like you're part of a community working toward the same goal.

Best for: People who thrive on accountability and community support.

Key Stats at a Glance

App	What It Does	Best For
Forest	Plants virtual trees when you stay off your phone	People who need motivation and visual rewards
Freedom	Blocks distracting apps and websites	People who struggle with self-control

StayFocusd	Limits time on distracting websites	People who do most of their phone use through a browser
Screen Time/Digital Wellbeing	Tracks screen time and sets app limits	People who want a simple, built-in solution
Offtime	Blocks apps, filters notifications, and auto-responds to messages	People who need to disconnect completely
Moment	Tracks screen time and offers coaching	People who want personalized tips and progress tracking
Flipd	Locks your phone and offers focus groups	People who thrive on accountability and community support

How to Get Started

Now that you know about these apps, how do you get started? Here are a few tips to help you choose the right one and make the most of it:

1. **Identify Your Biggest Distractions**: Before you choose an app, think about what's causing the most problems. Is it social media? Games? News sites? Knowing your biggest distractions will help you pick the right tool.

2. **Start Small**: If you're new to using these kinds of apps, start with something simple, like Screen Time or Digital Wellbeing. Once you're comfortable, you can try more advanced tools like Freedom or Forest.

3. **Set Realistic Goals**: Don't try to cut your screen time in half overnight. Start with small, achievable goals, like reducing your social media use by 30 minutes a day.

4. **Track Your Progress**: Use the tracking features in these apps to see how much time you're saving. Celebrate your progress, no matter how small.

5. **Be Patient**: Breaking free from phone addiction takes time. Don't get discouraged if you slip up—just refocus and keep going.

Real-Life Examples

Let's look at a few real-life examples of how people have used these apps to reduce their phone use:

1. **Emma's Story**: Emma used to spend hours scrolling through Instagram every night. To break the habit, she started using Forest. She set a goal to stay off her phone for

30 minutes at a time, and over time, she was able to reduce her social media use by half.

2. **James's Story**: James realized that he was constantly checking his phone during work, which made it hard to stay focused. He started using Freedom to block distracting apps during work hours. As a result, he was able to get more done in less time.

3. **Sophia's Story**: Sophia wanted to spend more quality time with her family, but her phone was always getting in the way. She started using Offtime to block apps during dinner and family time. Over time, she found that she was more present and connected with her loved ones.

◆ Leveraging Technology to Beat Technology

It might sound a little strange, but sometimes the best way to fight technology is with more technology. Yes, our phones and apps are designed to keep us hooked, but there are also tools and features that can help us take back control. From screen time trackers to app blockers, technology can be a powerful ally in the fight against phone addiction.

The key is to use these tools wisely. Instead of letting your phone control you, you can use technology to set boundaries, stay focused, and create a healthier relationship with your devices. So, let's dive into how you can leverage technology to beat technology—and take back control of your time and attention.

Why Use Technology to Fight Phone Addiction?

Before we get into the specific tools, let's talk about why this approach works. Our phones are designed to be addictive. They're packed with features like endless scrolling, push notifications, and personalized algorithms that keep us coming back for more. But the same technology that keeps us hooked can also help us break free.

A 2023 report by *DataReportal* found that the average person spends **7 hours a day** on their phone. That's almost half of your waking hours! And much of that time is spent on apps that don't add much value to your life—social media, games, and other distractions. By using technology to set boundaries and track your usage, you can reclaim some of that time and use it for things that truly matter.

Tools to Help You Beat Phone Addiction

Here are some of the best tools and features you can use to take control of your phone use:

1. Screen Time Trackers

What they do: Screen time trackers, like the built-in features on iPhones (Screen Time) and Android phones (Digital Wellbeing), show you how much time you're spending on your phone and which apps you're using the most. They also let you set daily limits for specific apps and schedule downtime.

Why they work: These tools give you a clear picture of your phone habits, so you can see where you're spending too much time. Once you know where the problem areas are, you can take steps to cut back.

How to use them:

- Check your screen time report every day to see which apps you're using the most.

- Set daily limits for apps that you want to use less, like social media or games.

- Schedule downtime during times when you want to focus, like work hours or family time.

2. App Blockers

What they do: App blockers, like Freedom and StayFocusd, let you block distracting apps and websites for set periods of time. You can create custom blocklists, schedule focus sessions, and even sync your settings across multiple devices.

Why they work: App blockers take the temptation out of the equation by blocking access to distracting apps altogether. It's like putting a lock on your phone's most addictive features.

How to use them:

- Identify your biggest distractions (like social media or news sites) and add them to your blocklist.

- Schedule focus sessions during times when you need to concentrate, like work or study hours.

- Use the "lock" feature to prevent yourself from changing the settings during a focus session.

3. Focus Apps

What they do: Focus apps, like Forest and Flipd, help you stay focused by turning staying off your phone into a game or challenge. For example, Forest lets you plant a virtual tree that grows when you stay off your phone, while Flipd lets you join focus groups and challenges.

Why they work: These apps make staying off your phone fun and rewarding. The visual rewards and community support can motivate you to stay focused and reduce your screen time.

How to use them:

- Set a timer for a focus session and commit to staying off your phone until the timer runs out.

- Use the visual rewards (like growing a tree in Forest) to track your progress and stay motivated.

- Join focus groups or challenges to stay accountable and connect with others who are working toward the same goal.

4. Notification Management

What it does: Most phones let you customize your notifications, so you only get alerts for the things that really matter. You can turn off non-essential notifications, group notifications by app, and even set "Do Not Disturb" modes.

Why it works: Notifications are one of the biggest triggers for phone use. By reducing the number of notifications you get, you can reduce the urge to check your phone constantly.

How to use it:

- Go through your notification settings and turn off non-essential alerts, like social media updates or game notifications.

- Use "Do Not Disturb" mode during times when you need to focus, like work hours or bedtime.

- Group notifications by app, so you can check them all at once instead of being interrupted throughout the day.

5. Grayscale Mode

What it does: Grayscale mode turns your phone's screen black and white, making it less visually appealing and reducing the urge to scroll.

Why it works: Our brains are drawn to bright, colorful screens. By turning your phone to grayscale, you can make it less enticing and reduce the amount of time you spend on it.

How to use it:

- Go to your phone's settings and enable grayscale mode (on iPhones, it's under Accessibility > Display & Text Size > Color Filters).

- Use grayscale mode during times when you want to reduce your phone use, like in the evening or on weekends.

- Combine grayscale mode with other tools, like app blockers or focus apps, for even better results.

Key Stats at a Glance

Tool	What It Does	Best For
Screen Time Trackers	Tracks screen time and sets app limits	People who want to see where their time is going
App Blockers	Blocks distracting apps and websites	People who struggle with self-control
Focus Apps	Turns staying off your phone into a game or challenge	People who need motivation and visual rewards

Notification Management	Customizes notifications to reduce interruptions	People who are constantly distracted by alerts
Grayscale Mode	Turns your phone's screen black and white	People who want to make their phone less visually appealing

How to Get Started

Now that you know about these tools, how do you get started? Here are a few tips to help you choose the right ones and make the most of them:

1. **Identify Your Biggest Distractions**: Before you choose a tool, think about what's causing the most problems. Is it social media? Games? Notifications? Knowing your biggest distractions will help you pick the right tools.

2. **Start Small**: If you're new to using these kinds of tools, start with something simple, like Screen Time or notification management. Once you're comfortable, you can try more advanced tools like app blockers or focus apps.

3. **Set Realistic Goals**: Don't try to cut your screen time in half overnight. Start with small, achievable goals, like reducing your social media use by 30 minutes a day.

4. **Track Your Progress**: Use the tracking features in these tools to see how much time you're saving. Celebrate your progress, no matter how small.

5. **Be Patient**: Breaking free from phone addiction takes time. Don't get discouraged if you slip up—just refocus and keep going.

Real-Life Examples

Let's look at a few real-life examples of how people have used these tools to reduce their phone use:

1. **Emma's Story**: Emma used to spend hours scrolling through Instagram every night. To break the habit, she started using Screen Time to set a daily limit for the app. Over time, she was able to reduce her social media use by half.

2. **James's Story**: James realized that he was constantly checking his phone during work, which made it hard to stay focused. He started using Freedom to block distracting apps during work hours. As a result, he was able to get more done in less time.

3. **Sophia's Story**: Sophia wanted to spend more quality time with her family, but her phone was always getting in the way. She started using grayscale mode and notification management to reduce her phone use during family time. Over time, she found that she was more present and connected with her loved ones.

◆ Enlisting Support: Friends, Family, and Accountability

Breaking free from phone addiction isn't something you have to do alone. In fact, one of the most powerful ways to succeed is by enlisting the support of the people around you—your friends, family, and even coworkers. When you have a team cheering you on, holding you accountable, and sharing the journey with you, it's easier to stay motivated and stick to your goals.

Think about it: when you're trying to make a big change, like reducing your phone use, it's easy to feel overwhelmed or discouraged. But when you have someone by your side—someone who understands what you're going through and wants to help— it makes the process feel less daunting. So, let's talk about how you can enlist support from the people in your life and create a network of accountability to help you break free from phone addiction.

Why Support Matters

Before we dive into how to get support, let's talk about why it's so important. Breaking a habit like phone addiction is hard. It takes time, effort, and a lot of willpower. And when you're doing it alone, it's easy to slip back into old patterns.

But when you have support, you're more likely to succeed. A 2021 study by the *American Psychological Association* found that people who had social support were **50% more likely** to achieve their goals than those who tried to go it alone. Why? Because support gives you motivation, accountability, and a sense of connection. It reminds you that you're not alone in this journey.

How to Enlist Support

Here are some practical ways to get the support you need from friends, family, and even coworkers:

1. Share Your Goals

The first step is to let the people in your life know what you're trying to do. Be honest about your struggles with phone addiction and explain why you want to make a change. For example, you might say something like:

- "I've noticed that I'm spending way too much time on my phone, and it's affecting my mental health. I want to cut back, but I could really use your support."

- "I'm trying to be more present with my family, and that means spending less time on my phone. Can you help me stay accountable?"

When you share your goals, you're not just asking for help—you're also making a commitment. It's harder to give up when you know other people are rooting for you.

2. Find an Accountability Partner

An accountability partner is someone who checks in with you regularly to see how you're doing. This could be a friend, family member, or coworker who's also trying to reduce their phone use. You can set up regular check-ins, like a weekly phone call or coffee date, to talk about your progress and challenges.

For example, **Lisa** and her best friend **Maya** decided to become accountability partners. They both wanted to spend less time on social media, so they set a goal to limit their use to 30 minutes a day. Every Sunday, they would meet for coffee and talk about how the week went. If one of them slipped up, the other would offer encouragement and help them get back on track.

3. Create a Phone-Free Zone with Family

If you live with family, one of the best ways to reduce phone use is to create phone-free zones or times. For example, you might decide that phones aren't allowed at the dinner table or during family game night. This not only helps you cut back on screen time but also strengthens your relationships.

For example, **David** and his wife **Sarah** decided to make their bedroom a phone-free zone. They started charging their phones in the living room overnight and using an old-fashioned alarm clock instead. Over time, they found that they slept better and felt more connected to each other.

4. Join a Support Group

If you don't have someone in your immediate circle who can support you, consider joining a support group. There are many online communities and forums where people share their experiences with phone addiction and offer advice and encouragement. You can also look for local groups or workshops focused on digital wellness.

For example, **Jake** joined an online support group for people trying to reduce their screen time. He found it helpful to connect with others who were going through the same struggles and to share tips and strategies for staying off their phones.

5. Involve Your Coworkers

If your phone use is affecting your work, consider enlisting the support of your coworkers. You might suggest a team challenge to reduce screen time during work hours or create a shared accountability system.

For example, **Emily** and her coworkers decided to do a "phone-free Friday" challenge. Every Friday, they would leave their phones in a drawer during work hours and focus on being present and productive. They found that not only did they get more work done, but they also felt less stressed and more connected as a team.

Key Stats at a Glance

Benefits of Support	Details
Increased likelihood of success	50% more likely to achieve goals with social support (APA, 2021)
Improved mental health	Social support reduces stress and anxiety (Psychology Today, 2020)
Stronger relationships	Phone-free time improves family and coworker connections
Accountability	Regular check-ins help you stay on track

Real-Life Examples of Enlisting Support

Let's look at a few real-life examples of how people have enlisted support to reduce their phone use:

1. **Anna's Story**: Anna wanted to spend less time on her phone and more time with her kids. She talked to her husband, **Mark,** about her goals, and they decided to create a phone-free zone in their living room. Every

evening after dinner, they would leave their phones in the kitchen and spend an hour playing games or reading with their kids. Over time, Anna found that she felt more present and connected with her family.

2. **Tom's Story**: Tom realized that he was spending too much time on social media, especially during work hours. He talked to his coworker, **Rachel**, and they decided to become accountability partners. They set a goal to limit their social media use to 30 minutes a day and checked in with each other every Friday to talk about their progress. Tom found that having someone to hold him accountable made it easier to stick to his goals.

3. **Sophie's Story**: Sophie joined an online support group for people trying to reduce their screen time. She found it helpful to connect with others who were going through the same struggles and to share tips and strategies for staying off their phones. Over time, Sophie was able to cut her screen time in half and felt more in control of her phone use.

How to Be a Good Support System

If someone in your life is trying to reduce their phone use, here are a few ways you can support them:

1. **Be Encouraging**: Offer words of encouragement and celebrate their progress, no matter how small.

2. **Be Patient**: Breaking a habit takes time, so be patient and understanding if they slip up.

3. **Lead by Example**: If you're also trying to reduce your phone use, share your own experiences and challenges.

4. **Create Phone-Free Activities**: Suggest activities that don't involve phones, like going for a walk, playing a game, or having a conversation.

Your Turn: Build Your Support Network

♦ Now it's your turn. Who in your life can you enlist to support you in breaking free from phone addiction? Maybe it's a friend, family member, or coworker. Whatever it is, remember: you don't have to do this alone. With the right support, you can create a healthier, more balanced relationship with technology.

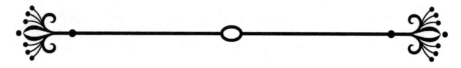

Chapter 3: Thriving After the Breakup

◆ 3.1 Redefining Your Relationship with Technology

Let's face it: our phones are incredibly powerful tools. They help us stay connected, get work done, and access information in ways that were unimaginable just a few decades ago. But somewhere along the way, many of us started using our phones as a crutch— something we rely on too much, even when it's not necessary. Instead of using our phones to enhance our lives, we've let them take over.

The good news is, it doesn't have to be this way. By shifting our mindset and using our phones as tools rather than crutches, we can create a healthier, more balanced relationship with technology. So, let's talk about how to do that—and how to practice mindful tech habits for long-term success.

What Does It Mean to Use Your Phone as a Tool?

Using your phone as a tool means being intentional about how and when you use it. It's about recognizing that your phone is there to serve you, not the other way around. Instead of mindlessly scrolling or constantly checking for updates, you use your phone for specific purposes that add value to your life.

For example:

- **Communication**: Using your phone to stay in touch with loved ones or collaborate with coworkers.

- **Productivity**: Using apps to manage your schedule, take notes, or track your goals.

- **Learning**: Using your phone to read articles, listen to podcasts, or take online courses.

- **Convenience**: Using your phone for navigation, online shopping, or quick information searches.

- The key is to use your phone with purpose, rather than letting it control your time and attention.

How to Shift from Crutch to Tool

Here are some practical steps to help you use your phone as a tool, not a crutch:

1. Set Clear Intentions

Before you pick up your phone, ask yourself: *Why am I using this right now?* Is it for a specific purpose, or are you just bored or avoiding something? By setting clear intentions, you can reduce mindless scrolling and focus on using your phone in ways that add value.

For example, **Maria** used to spend hours scrolling through social media every night. She realized she was using her phone as a way to avoid thinking about her stressful day. To break the habit, she started setting a clear intention before using her phone: "I'm going to check my messages and then put it down." Over time, she found that she was spending less time on her phone and more time relaxing in healthier ways.

2. Organize Your Apps

One way to use your phone as a tool is to organize your apps by purpose. For example, you might have folders for work, health, entertainment, and social media. This makes it easier to access the apps you need and avoid the ones that waste your time.

For example, **John** organized his phone into folders like "Work," "Fitness," and "Social." He moved his most distracting apps, like games and social media, to a folder called "Limit." By making these apps harder to access, he found that he was less likely to open them out of habit.

3. Turn Off Non-Essential Notifications

Notifications are one of the biggest distractions on your phone. By turning off non-essential notifications, you can reduce the urge to check your phone constantly and focus on using it as a tool.

For example, **Sophie** turned off notifications for all her social media apps and email. She only allowed notifications for calls and texts from family and close friends. As a result, she found that she was less distracted and more focused throughout the day.

4. Schedule Tech-Free Time

Another way to use your phone as a tool is to schedule regular tech-free time. This could be during meals, before bed, or on weekends. By setting boundaries, you can create space for other activities and reduce your reliance on your phone.

For example, **Carlos** and his family decided to make dinner time a phone-free zone. They started leaving their phones in another room during meals and found that they were more present and connected with each other.

Mindful Tech Practices for Long-Term Success

Using your phone as a tool is a great start, but to create a lasting change, you need to practice mindful tech habits. Here are some tips to help you do that:

1. Practice Digital Minimalism

Digital minimalism is the idea of using technology intentionally and only keeping the tools that add value to your life. This means deleting apps you don't need, unsubscribing from unnecessary emails, and simplifying your digital life.

For example, **Emma** decided to practice digital minimalism by deleting all the apps she didn't use regularly. She also unsubscribed from email newsletters and turned off notifications for non-essential apps. Over time, she found that her phone felt less cluttered and more manageable.

2. Use Mindfulness Techniques

Mindfulness is the practice of being fully present in the moment. By applying mindfulness to your tech use, you can reduce distractions and stay focused on what's important.

For example, **Liam** started practicing mindfulness by taking a few deep breaths before using his phone. He also set a timer for 10 minutes when he needed to check social media, so he didn't get sucked into endless scrolling.

3. Reflect on Your Tech Use

Regularly reflecting on your tech use can help you stay mindful and make adjustments as needed. At the end of each day or week, ask yourself:

- How much time did I spend on my phone?
- Did I use my phone as a tool or a crutch?
- What could I do differently next time?

For example, **Nina** started keeping a journal to track her phone use and reflect on her habits. She found that writing things down helped her stay accountable and make better choices.

4. Create Tech-Free Rituals

Creating tech-free rituals can help you build healthier habits and reduce your reliance on your phone. For example, you might start your day with a tech-free morning routine or end your day with a tech-free wind-down.

For example, **Alex** decided to start his day with a tech-free morning routine. Instead of checking his phone first thing, he would meditate, exercise, and eat breakfast without any screens. He found that this helped him feel more focused and energized throughout the day.

Key Stats at a Glance

Mindful Tech Practices	Benefits
Digital minimalism	Reduces clutter and distractions, simplifies digital life
Mindfulness techniques	Improves focus, reduces stress, and increases self-awareness
Reflecting on tech use	Helps you stay accountable and make better choices
Tech-free rituals	Creates space for other activities and reduces reliance on phones

Real-Life Examples of Mindful Tech Use

Let's look at a few real-life examples of how people have used their phones as tools and practiced mindful tech habits:

1. **Sarah's Story**: Sarah used to spend hours on her phone every night, scrolling through social media and watching videos. To break the habit, she started practicing digital minimalism. She deleted all the apps she didn't need and set a daily limit for social media. Over time, she found that she was spending less time on her phone and more time reading and relaxing.

2. **Mike's Story**: Mike realized that he was constantly checking his phone during work, which made it hard to stay focused. He started using mindfulness techniques, like taking deep breaths before using his phone and setting a timer for 10 minutes when he needed to check email. As a result, he was able to get more done in less time.

3. **Emily's Story**: Emily wanted to spend more quality time with her family, but her phone was always getting in the way. She started creating tech-free rituals, like leaving her phone in another room during dinner and spending an hour each evening playing games with her kids. Over time, she found that she was more present and connected with her loved ones.

Your Turn: Use Your Phone as a Tool

Now it's your turn. How can you start using your phone as a tool, not a crutch? Maybe it's setting clear intentions, organizing your apps, or practicing mindfulness. Whatever it is, remember: the goal isn't to give up your phone completely—it's to create a healthier, more balanced relationship with technology. You've got this.

3.2 Rediscovering Joy and Presence

Let's talk about something that often gets pushed aside when we're glued to our phones: the things that truly matter. Hobbies, passions, and in-person connections are the things that make life rich and meaningful. They're the moments that bring us joy, help us grow, and remind us of what's important. But when we're constantly scrolling, texting, or checking notifications, these things can easily fall by the wayside.

The good news is, when you break free from phone addiction, you reclaim time for what matters most. You can rediscover old hobbies, explore new passions, and deepen your connections with the people around you. So, let's dive into how you can make space for these things in your life—and why they're worth it.

Why Hobbies and Passions Matter

Hobbies and passions aren't just fun—they're essential for our well-being. They give us a sense of purpose, help us relax, and allow us to express ourselves in creative ways. Whether it's painting, playing an instrument, gardening, or cooking, hobbies give us a break from the stresses of everyday life and help us recharge.

A 2021 study by the *University of London* found that people who regularly engaged in hobbies reported higher levels of happiness and life satisfaction. Hobbies also reduce stress, improve mental health, and even boost creativity. But here's the catch: when we're spending hours on our phones every day, we often don't have the time or energy to pursue these activities.

How to Rediscover Your Hobbies and Passions

If you've been neglecting your hobbies or feel like you don't have any, don't worry—it's never too late to start. Here are some tips to help you rediscover your passions:

1. Think Back to What You Loved

Start by thinking about the things you used to love doing before your phone took over. Did you used to paint, play sports, or write stories? Revisiting old hobbies can be a great way to reconnect with your passions.

For example, **Anna** used to love painting when she was younger, but she hadn't picked up a brush in years. After realizing how much time she was wasting on her phone, she decided to start painting again. She set aside an hour every weekend to work on a new piece, and over time, she found that painting brought her a sense of joy and fulfillment she had been missing.

2. Try Something New

If you're not sure what you're passionate about, try something new. Take a class, join a club, or just experiment with different activities until you find something you enjoy. You might discover a hidden talent or a new passion you never knew you had.

For example, **Jake** had always been curious about photography but never had the time to try it. After cutting back on his phone use, he signed up for a beginner's photography class. He found that he loved capturing moments and exploring his creativity through photos.

3. Make Time for Your Hobbies

Once you've identified your hobbies or passions, make time for them. Schedule regular blocks of time in your week to focus on these activities, and treat them as non-negotiable. Remember, this is your time to recharge and do something you love.

For example, **Sophie** decided to dedicate every Wednesday evening to her passion for baking. She would try out new recipes, experiment with flavors, and share her creations with friends and family. Over time, baking became a cherished part of her routine.

The Power of In-Person Connections

While hobbies and passions are important, nothing beats the power of in-person connections. Spending time with loved ones, having meaningful conversations, and sharing experiences are what make life truly fulfilling. But when we're constantly on our phones, these connections can suffer.

A 2021 survey by *Pew Research Center* found that **51% of people** said their partner was distracted by their phone during conversations. And it's not just romantic relationships—friends, family members, and coworkers can also feel ignored or unimportant when we prioritize our phones over them.

How to Strengthen In-Person Connections

Here are some ways to deepen your connections with the people around you:

1. Be Fully Present

When you're spending time with someone, put your phone away and be fully present. Listen actively, make eye contact, and engage in the conversation. This simple act can make a big difference in how connected you feel.

For example, **Carlos** realized that he was always checking his phone during family dinners, which made it hard to connect with his kids. He started leaving his phone in another room during meals and found that he was more present and engaged with his family.

2. Plan Phone-Free Activities

Plan activities that don't involve phones, like going for a walk, playing a board game, or having a picnic. These activities create opportunities for meaningful connections and shared experiences.

For example, **Emma** and her friends decided to start a monthly book club. They would meet in person to discuss the book, share snacks, and catch up on each other's lives. Over time, the book club became a cherished tradition that brought them closer together.

3. Schedule Regular Check-Ins

Life can get busy, but it's important to make time for the people who matter most. Schedule regular check-ins with friends and family, whether it's a weekly phone call, a monthly dinner, or a yearly trip.

For example, **Liam** and his best friend **Ryan** live in different cities, but they make it a point to have a video call every Sunday. They catch up on each other's lives, share stories, and offer support. These regular check-ins help them stay connected despite the distance.

Reclaiming Time for What Matters Most

When you break free from phone addiction, you reclaim time for the things that truly matter—hobbies, passions, and in-person connections. But how do you make the most of that time? Here are some tips:

1. Prioritize What's Important

Take a moment to think about what's most important to you. Is it spending time with family? Pursuing a creative passion?

Volunteering in your community? Once you know what matters most, make it a priority in your life.

For example, **Nina** realized that spending time with her grandmother was one of her top priorities. She started visiting her every Sunday afternoon, and they would bake cookies, look through old photo albums, and share stories. These visits became a highlight of Nina's week.

2. Set Boundaries with Your Phone

To reclaim time for what matters most, you need to set boundaries with your phone. Turn off non-essential notifications, set daily screen time limits, and create phone-free zones in your home.

For example, **Tom** decided to make his living room a phone-free zone. He started leaving his phone in the kitchen when he was spending time with his family, and he found that he was more present and engaged with his loved ones.

3. Celebrate Small Wins

Breaking free from phone addiction is a journey, and it's important to celebrate your progress along the way. Whether it's spending an hour on a hobby, having a meaningful conversation, or simply enjoying some quiet time, take a moment to appreciate these small wins.

For example, **Sophia** started keeping a gratitude journal to track her progress. Every night, she would write down one thing she was grateful for, like spending time with her kids or finishing a painting. Over time, she found that this practice helped her stay motivated and focused on what mattered most.

Key Stats at a Glance

Benefits of Hobbies and Connections	Details
Happiness and life satisfaction	Higher levels reported by people with hobbies (University of London, 2021)
Stress reduction	Hobbies reduce stress and improve mental health
Relationship strength	51% say phones distract during conversations (Pew Research, 2021)
Time reclaimed	Average person spends 7 hours/day on their phone (DataReportal, 2023)

Real-Life Examples of Reclaiming Time

- Let's look at a few real-life examples of how people have reclaimed time for what matters most:

1. **Maria's Story**: Maria used to spend hours on her phone every night, scrolling through social media and watching videos. After realizing how much time she was wasting, she decided to start painting again. She set aside an hour every weekend to work on a new piece, and over time, she found that painting brought her a sense of joy and fulfillment she had been missing.

2. **David's Story**: David realized that he was always checking his phone during family dinners, which made it hard to connect with his kids. He started leaving his phone in another room during meals and found that he was more present and engaged with his family.

3. **Sophie's Story**: Sophie and her friends decided to start a monthly book club. They would meet in person to discuss the book, share snacks, and catch up on each other's lives. Over time, the book club became a cherished tradition that brought them closer together.

Your Turn: Reclaim Your Time

Now it's your turn. What hobbies, passions, or connections have you been neglecting? How can you reclaim time for what matters most? Whether it's picking up a paintbrush, planning a phone-free activity with friends, or simply enjoying some quiet time, remember: the time you spend on what truly matters is never wasted.

♦ <u>3.3 Celebrating Your Freedom</u>

Breaking free from phone addiction is a journey, not a one-time event. Along the way, you'll experience moments of triumph, setbacks, and everything in between. The key is to measure your progress, stay committed even when you slip, and inspire others to join you on the path to a healthier relationship with technology. Let's dive into how you can do all three—and why it's worth it.

Measuring Progress: How Life Feels Without the Chains

When you start reducing your phone use, you'll notice changes— big and small. Maybe you'll feel less stressed, sleep better, or have more time for the things you love. These changes are signs that you're making progress, and they're worth celebrating.

But how do you measure that progress? Here are some ways to track how life feels without the chains of phone addiction:

1. Track Your Screen Time

Most smartphones have built-in tools to track your screen time, like Screen Time on iPhones and Digital Wellbeing on Android. Use these tools to see how much time you're saving and which apps you're using less. Over time, you'll see a clear picture of your progress.

For example, **Sarah** used Screen Time to track her phone use. At first, she was spending 6 hours a day on her phone, mostly on social media. After setting daily limits and creating phone-free zones, she reduced her screen time to 3 hours a day. She felt more in control and had more time for her hobbies.

2. Reflect on How You Feel

Take a moment each week to reflect on how you're feeling. Are you less stressed? More present? Sleeping better? Write down your thoughts in a journal or share them with a friend. This reflection can help you see the positive changes in your life.

For example, **Mike** started keeping a journal to track his progress. Every Sunday, he would write about how he felt that week—whether he was more focused at work, more connected with his family, or just happier overall. Over time, he noticed a clear improvement in his mental health and well-being.

3. Celebrate Small Wins

Breaking free from phone addiction is a big achievement, but it's made up of small wins along the way. Celebrate those wins, no matter how small. Did you spend an hour less on your phone today? Did you have a meaningful conversation without checking your phone? These are all signs of progress.

For example, **Emily** decided to celebrate her small wins by treating herself to something she loved, like a cup of her favorite coffee or a walk in the park. These little rewards kept her motivated and reminded her of how far she had come.

Staying Committed: What to Do If You Slip

Let's be real: breaking free from phone addiction isn't easy, and there will be times when you slip up. Maybe you'll spend hours scrolling through social media one day, or you'll check your phone during a family dinner. That's okay. What matters is how you respond.

Here's what to do if you slip:

1. Don't Beat Yourself Up

Slipping up doesn't mean you've failed. It's just part of the process. Instead of beating yourself up, remind yourself that progress isn't linear. Everyone has setbacks, and what matters is that you keep going.

For example, **Carlos** had a busy week at work and found himself spending more time on his phone than usual. Instead of feeling guilty, he reminded himself that it was just a temporary setback. He refocused on his goals and got back on track the following week.

2. Identify What Went Wrong

Take a moment to reflect on why you slipped. Were you stressed? Bored? Tired? Understanding the root cause can help you avoid the same mistake in the future.

For example, **Sophie** realized that she was spending more time on her phone when she was feeling overwhelmed at work. To address this, she started practicing mindfulness techniques, like deep breathing and meditation, to manage her stress without turning to her phone.

3. Revisit Your Goals

If you slip up, it's a good time to revisit your goals. Are they realistic? Do they still align with what you want to achieve? Adjust your goals if needed, and remind yourself why you're doing this in the first place.

For example, **Jake** realized that his goal of spending only 1 hour a day on his phone was too ambitious. He adjusted his goal to 2 hours a day and found that it was more manageable. Over time, he was able to reduce his screen time even further.

4. Get Back on Track

Once you've reflected on what went wrong and revisited your goals, it's time to get back on track. Start fresh, and don't let one slip-up derail your progress.

For example, **Anna** had a day where she spent hours scrolling through social media. Instead of giving up, she decided to start fresh the next day. She turned off notifications, set a daily limit for social media, and focused on being more present.

Inspiring Others to Break Free

Once you've made progress in breaking free from phone addiction, you might feel inspired to help others do the same. Sharing your journey can not only inspire others but also reinforce your own commitment to a healthier relationship with technology.

Here's how you can inspire others to break free:

1. Lead by Example

The best way to inspire others is to lead by example. Show your friends and family what's possible by living a more balanced, phone-free life. When they see the positive changes in your life, they might be inspired to make changes too.

For example, **Liam** started leaving his phone in another room during family dinners and spending more time on his hobbies. His wife noticed the positive changes and decided to join him in reducing her phone use.

2. Share Your Story

Share your journey with others—whether it's through a conversation, a blog post, or a social media update. Be honest about your struggles and successes, and offer tips and advice for others who want to break free.

For example, **Nina** started a blog to share her journey of breaking free from phone addiction. She wrote about her challenges, her progress, and the tools that helped her along the way. Her blog inspired many readers to take steps toward a healthier relationship with technology.

3. Offer Support

If someone in your life is struggling with phone addiction, offer your support. Share the tools and strategies that worked for you, and encourage them to set small, achievable goals.

For example, **Tom** noticed that his coworker **Rachel** was always on her phone during meetings. He shared his experience of using app blockers and setting daily limits, and Rachel decided to give it a try. Over time, she found that she was more focused and productive at work.

Key Stats at a Glance

Measuring Progress	Details
Screen time reduction	Average person spends 7 hours/day on their phone (DataReportal, 2023)
Mental health improvement	Reduced stress and anxiety with less phone use (Psychology Today, 2021)
Relationship strength	51% say phones distract during conversations (Pew Research, 2021)
Staying Committed	**Details**

Progress isn't linear	Setbacks are normal; focus on getting back on track
Mindfulness techniques	Help manage stress and reduce phone use
Adjusting goals	Make goals realistic and achievable

Inspiring Others	**Details**
Leading by example	Show others the benefits of a phone-free life
Sharing your story	Inspire others through honesty and vulnerability
Offering support	Help others set goals and stay accountable

Real-Life Examples of Progress and Commitment

Let's look at a few real-life examples of how people have measured their progress, stayed committed, and inspired others:

1. **Emma's Story**: Emma used Screen Time to track her phone use and reduced her screen time from 6 hours a day to 3 hours. She celebrated her small wins by treating herself to her favorite coffee and inspired her friend **Sophie** to start reducing her phone use too.

2. **Mike's Story**: Mike slipped up during a busy week at work but didn't beat himself up. He reflected on what went wrong, adjusted his goals, and got back on track. Over time, he found that he was more focused and less stressed.

3. **Liam's Story**: Liam led by example by leaving his phone in another room during family dinners and spending more time on his hobbies. His wife noticed the positive changes and decided to join him in reducing her phone use.

Your Turn: Measure, Commit, Inspire

Now it's your turn. How will you measure your progress? What will you do if you slip? And how can you inspire others to break free from phone addiction? Remember, this is a journey, and every step you take brings you closer to a healthier, more balanced life. You've got this.

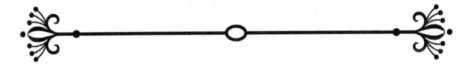

Conclusion

Imagine this: a life where your phone doesn't control you. A life where you have time for the things you love—hobbies, passions, and meaningful connections. A life where you feel present, focused, and free. This is the life you're building as you break free from phone addiction. It's not always easy, but it's worth it. And you're not alone. More and more people are joining the movement toward **tech-life balance**, where technology serves us instead of controlling us.

So, let's take a moment to celebrate your new life and explore how this movement is growing. This is your love letter to the life you're creating—and to the future you're helping shape.

◆ A Love Letter to Your New Life

Dear You,

I see you. I see the effort you're putting into breaking free from phone addiction. I see the small wins, the setbacks, and the moments of clarity when you realize how much better life feels without the constant pull of your phone.

I see the mornings you wake up and don't immediately reach for your phone. Instead, you stretch, breathe, and maybe even enjoy a quiet cup of coffee. I see the dinners where you're fully present with your family, laughing and talking without the distraction of notifications. I see the hobbies you've rediscovered—the painting, the gardening, the reading—and the joy they bring you.

This new life isn't perfect, and it's not always easy. There are days when you slip up, when you find yourself mindlessly scrolling or checking your phone out of habit. But you don't let those moments define you. You get back up, refocus, and keep going.

This new life is about more than just using your phone less. It's about reclaiming your time, your attention, and your joy. It's about being present in the moments that matter—whether it's a conversation with a friend, a walk in nature, or just a quiet moment alone.

So, keep going. Keep celebrating the small wins. Keep learning from the setbacks. And most importantly, keep loving this new life you're creating. You deserve it.

With love,
Your Future Self

The Movement Toward Tech-Life Balance

You're not just changing your own life—you're part of a bigger movement. More and more people are waking up to the reality that technology, while amazing, can also take over our lives if we let it. The movement toward **tech-life balance** is about finding a healthy relationship with technology—one where it serves us instead of controlling us.

Here's how this movement is growing and why it matters:

Why Tech-Life Balance Matters

Tech-life balance isn't about giving up technology completely. It's about using it intentionally and making sure it enhances our lives instead of detracting from them. Here's why this balance is so important:

1. **Mental Health**: Constant phone use can lead to stress, anxiety, and even depression. A 2022 study by the *Journal of Social and Clinical Psychology* found that people who spent more than **2 hours a day** on social media were **three times more likely** to feel depressed or anxious. By finding balance, we can protect our mental health.

2. **Relationships**: Our phones can strain our relationships if we're not careful. A 2021 survey by *Pew Research Center* found that **51% of people** said their partner was distracted by their phone during conversations. Tech-life balance helps us be more present with the people we care about.

3. **Productivity**: Our phones are designed to distract us, and that can take a toll on our productivity. Research from the *University of California, Irvine* found that it takes an

average of **23 minutes** to refocus after a distraction. By setting boundaries with our phones, we can get more done in less time.

4. **Joy and Fulfillment**: When we're not constantly glued to our phones, we have more time for the things that truly matter—hobbies, passions, and in-person connections. These are the things that bring us joy and make life meaningful.

How the Movement Is Growing

The movement toward tech-life balance is gaining momentum. Here are some ways it's growing:

1. Digital Detox Retreats

More and more people are signing up for digital detox retreats, where they can unplug and reconnect with themselves and the world around them. These retreats offer a chance to step away from technology and focus on mindfulness, nature, and human connection.

For example, **Sarah** attended a digital detox retreat in the mountains. She spent a weekend without her phone, hiking, meditating, and connecting with other participants. When she returned home, she felt refreshed and inspired to create more balance in her daily life.

2. Tech-Free Zones

Schools, workplaces, and even restaurants are creating tech-free zones to encourage people to be more present. For example, some schools have implemented phone-free classrooms, while some restaurants offer discounts to customers who leave their phones at the door.

For example, **Mike** works at a company that has designated phone-free meeting rooms. He found that these meetings were more productive and focused, and he started implementing phone-free zones at home too.

3. Mindfulness and Tech

Mindfulness practices, like meditation and deep breathing, are becoming more popular as people look for ways to reduce stress and stay present. Many apps now offer mindfulness features, like guided meditations and breathing exercises, to help people find balance.

For example, **Emily** started using a mindfulness app to help her stay present and reduce her phone use. She found that the guided meditations helped her feel more calm and focused throughout the day.

4. Community Support

Online and in-person communities are forming to support people in their journey toward tech-life balance. These communities offer tips, encouragement, and accountability to help people stay on track.

For example, **Carlos** joined an online community for people trying to reduce their screen time. He found it helpful to connect with others who were going through the same struggles and to share tips and strategies.

Key Stats at a Glance

Tech-Life Balance Movement	Details
Mental health benefits	Reduced stress and anxiety with less phone use (Psychology Today, 2021)
Relationship strength	51% say phones distract during conversations (Pew Research, 2021)
Productivity boost	23 minutes to refocus after a distraction (University of California, 2018)
Digital detox retreats	Growing popularity as people seek to unplug and reconnect
Tech-free zones	Schools, workplaces, and restaurants creating phone-free spaces

Real-Life Examples of Tech-Life Balance

Let's look at a few real-life examples of how people are finding tech-life balance:

1. **Anna's Story**: Anna used to spend hours on her phone every night, scrolling through social media and watching videos. After attending a digital detox retreat, she started setting boundaries with her phone. She now spends her evenings reading, painting, and spending time with her family.

2. **Jake's Story**: Jake works at a company that has designated phone-free meeting rooms. He found that these meetings were more productive and focused, and he started implementing phone-free zones at home too. His family now enjoys phone-free dinners and game nights.

3. **Sophie's Story**: Sophie joined an online community for people trying to reduce their screen time. She found it helpful to connect with others who were going through the same struggles and to share tips and strategies. Over time, she was able to cut her screen time in half and feel more in control of her phone use.

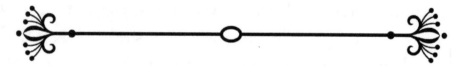

Resources

Breaking free from phone addiction is a journey, and like any journey, it helps to have the right resources and support along the way. Whether you're looking for more information, tools to help you stay on track, or a community to share your experiences with, this section has you covered. Let's dive into some recommended reads, helpful apps, and support groups that can guide you toward a healthier relationship with technology.

Recommended Reads and Studies on Phone Addiction

- If you want to dive deeper into the science and psychology of phone addiction, here are some books and studies that can help you understand the issue and find solutions:

1. *Digital Minimalism* by Cal Newport

- This book is a must-read for anyone looking to create a healthier relationship with technology. Cal Newport argues that we should be intentional about how we use technology, focusing only on the tools that add value to our lives. He offers practical tips for reducing screen time and reclaiming your attention.

- **Why it's helpful**: It provides a clear framework for using technology intentionally and offers actionable steps to reduce digital clutter.

2. *Irresistible: The Rise of Addictive Technology and the Business of Keeping Us Hooked* by Adam Alter

- Adam Alter explores how technology companies design apps and devices to keep us hooked. He also discusses the impact of phone addiction on our mental health and relationships, and offers strategies for breaking free.

- **Why it's helpful**: It gives you a behind-the-scenes look at how technology is designed to be addictive and offers insights into how to resist it.

3. *How to Break Up with Your Phone* by Catherine Price

- This book is a practical guide to reducing phone addiction. Catherine Price walks you through a 30-day plan to break free from your phone and create a healthier relationship with technology.

- **Why it's helpful**: It's a step-by-step guide with actionable tips and exercises to help you take control of your phone use.

4. *The Shallows: What the Internet Is Doing to Our Brains* by Nicholas Carr

- Nicholas Carr explores how the internet and constant connectivity are changing the way we think, read, and remember. He argues that our brains are being rewired by technology, and offers insights into how to protect our cognitive abilities.

- **Why it's helpful**: It helps you understand the long-term effects of phone addiction on your brain and offers strategies for preserving your focus and memory.

5. Key Studies on Phone Addiction

- Here are some key studies that shed light on the impact of phone addiction:

- **University of Pennsylvania (2018)**: Found that reducing social media use to 30 minutes a day significantly improved mental health.

- **Journal of Social and Clinical Psychology (2022)**: Linked excessive social media use to higher levels of anxiety and depression.

- **University of California, Irvine (2018)**: Found that it takes an average of 23 minutes to refocus after a phone distraction.

Tools and Apps Mentioned in the Book

- Throughout this book, we've talked about tools and apps that can help you reduce phone addiction and create a healthier relationship with technology. Here's a quick recap of the most helpful ones:

1. Forest

- **What it does**: Helps you stay focused by planting a virtual tree that grows when you stay off your phone.

- **Why it's helpful**: It turns staying off your phone into a game, with visual rewards that motivate you to stay focused.

2. Freedom

- **What it does**: Blocks distracting apps and websites for set periods of time.

- **Why it's helpful**: It removes the temptation to check your phone, helping you stay focused and productive.

3. StayFocusd

- **What it does**: Limits the amount of time you can spend on distracting websites.

- **Why it's helpful**: It forces you to be mindful of how much time you're spending online.

4. Screen Time (iOS) and Digital Wellbeing (Android)

- **What they do**: Track your screen time and set daily limits for specific apps.

- **Why they're helpful**: They give you a clear picture of your phone habits and help you set boundaries.

5. Offtime

- **What it does**: Blocks apps, filters notifications, and auto-responds to messages so you can focus without interruptions.

- **Why it's helpful**: It's perfect for creating strict boundaries around your phone use.

6. Moment

- **What it does**: Tracks your screen time and offers coaching to help you reduce it.

- **Why it's helpful**: It provides personalized tips and progress tracking to keep you motivated.

7. Flipd

- **What it does**: Locks your phone for set periods of time and offers focus groups for accountability.

- **Why it's helpful**: It's great for people who thrive on community support and accountability.

Further Support Groups and Communities

- Sometimes, the best way to stay on track is to connect with others who are going through the same journey. Here are some support groups and communities that can help you break free from phone addiction:

1. Online Communities

- **Reddit's r/nosurf**: A community of people working to reduce their screen time and break free from internet addiction.

- **Facebook Groups**: Search for groups focused on digital detox or tech-life balance. Many offer tips, encouragement, and accountability.

2. Local Meetups

- **Digital Detox Meetups**: Check out platforms like Meetup.com for local groups focused on reducing screen time and reconnecting with the real world.

- **Mindfulness and Meditation Groups**: Many mindfulness groups also focus on reducing tech use and being more present.

3. Workshops and Retreats

- **Digital Detox Retreats**: These retreats offer a chance to unplug and reconnect with yourself and nature. Many also offer workshops on mindfulness and tech-life balance.

- **Workshops on Tech-Life Balance**: Look for local or online workshops that teach strategies for reducing screen time and creating a healthier relationship with technology.

4. Accountability Partners

- **Find a Friend**: Ask a friend or family member to join you in reducing phone use. You can check in with each other regularly and offer support.

- **Online Accountability Partners**: Some online communities, like r/nosurf, offer accountability partner programs where you can connect with someone who shares your goals.

Key Stats at a Glance

Recommended Reads	Details
Digital Minimalism by Cal Newport	Focuses on intentional tech use and reducing digital clutter
Irresistible by Adam Alter	Explores how tech is designed to be addictive and how to resist it
How to Break Up with Your Phone	A 30-day plan to reduce phone addiction
The Shallows by Nicholas Carr	Examines how the internet is changing our brains
Tools and Apps	**Details**
Forest	Plants virtual trees when you stay off your phone

Freedom	Blocks distracting apps and websites
StayFocusd	Limits time on distracting websites
Screen Time/Digital Wellbeing	Tracks screen time and sets app limits
Offtime	Blocks apps and filters notifications
Moment	Tracks screen time and offers coaching
Flipd	Locks your phone and offers focus groups
Support Groups and Communities	**Details**
Reddit's r/nosurf	Online community for reducing screen time
Facebook Groups	Groups focused on digital detox and tech-life balance
Digital Detox Meetups	Local meetups for unplugging and reconnecting

Mindfulness Groups	Focus on reducing tech use and being present
Accountability Partners	Friends, family, or online partners for support and accountability

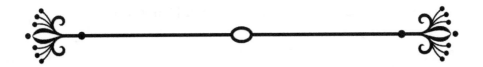

Before You Go

My final request...

Being a smaller author, reviews help me tremendously!

It would mean the world to me if you could leave a review.

Customer reviews

★★★★★ 5 out of 5

12 customer ratings

5 star		100%
4 star		0%
3 star		0%
2 star		0%
1 star		0%

˅ How does Amazon calculate star ratings?

Review this product

Share your thoughts with other customers

> Write a customer review

If you liked reading this book and enjoyed some of it, please go to this link:

>> Please go and leave a brief review on Amazon.

It only takes 30 seconds, but it means so much to me! Thank you, and I can't wait to see your thoughts.

Scroll No More

www.ingramcontent.com/pod-product-compliance
Lightning Source LLC
LaVergne TN
LVHW052100060326
832903LV00060B/2449